MW01134686

The New Addiction Treatment

The New Addiction Treatment

*From Good Intentions and Bad Intuitions
to Data, Performance, and Technology*

DAVID A. PATTERSON SILVER WOLF

OXFORD
UNIVERSITY PRESS

OXFORD
UNIVERSITY PRESS

Oxford University Press is a department of the University of Oxford. It furthers the University's objective of excellence in research, scholarship, and education by publishing worldwide. Oxford is a registered trade mark of Oxford University Press in the UK and certain other countries.

Published in the United States of America by Oxford University Press
198 Madison Avenue, New York, NY 10016, United States of America.

Library of Congress Cataloging-in-Publication Data
Names: David, Patterson Silver Wolf, author.
Title: The new addiction treatment: from good intentions and bad
intuitions to data, performance, and technology / Patterson Silver Wolf David.
Description: New York, NY : Oxford University Press, [2021] |
Includes bibliographical references and index.
Identifiers: LCCN 2021006595 (print) | LCCN 2021006596 (ebook) |
ISBN 9780197601372 (hardback) | ISBN 9780197601396 (epub) |
ISBN 9780197601402
Subjects: LCSH: Drug abuse—Treatment—United States. |
Drug addiction—Treatment—United States. |
Alcoholism—Treatment—United States.
Classification: LCC HV 5825 .D377 2021 (print) |
LCC HV 5825 (ebook) | DDC 616.86/060973—dc23
LC record available at https://lccn.loc.gov/2021006595
LC ebook record available at https://lccn.loc.gov/2021006596

DOI: 10.1093/oso/9780197601372.001.0001

1 3 5 7 9 8 6 4 2

Printed by Integrated Books International, United States of America

This book is dedicated to my wife, Nicole, and our three children,
Ambra, Conall, and Aidan.
My love. My life. My everything.

From Good Intentions and Bad Intuitions to Data, Performance and Technology

> *What goes on in Detox Mansion*
> *Outside the rubber room*
> *We get therapy and lectures*
> *We play golf in the afternoon*

Warren Zevon and Jorge Calderon
"Detox Mansion," 1987

Contents

Preface

Small annoyances sometimes grow into very big problems. In my life I've had two very big problems that have motivated me to write this book. One of them began with a cheap pair of shoes; the other began with a seemingly ordinary, garden-variety headache. Both problems required medical attention, but though the two problems were similarly life-threatening, the two treatments could not have been more different.

At the high school I attended in Louisville, Kentucky, in 1977, if you did not own a pair of Chucks, you were a loser, a chump. Converse Chuck Taylor All-Stars, or *Chucks* for short, were the gym shoes that conferred both status and acceptance. A pair of Chucks would not, by themselves, give you the keys to the high school kingdom, but, like straight teeth or clear skin, they were a prerequisite.

Unfortunately, my family was poor, and those shoes, like many other of life's prerequisites, were beyond our means.

My mom, sympathetic to the need to conform, urged me to wear the Kmart brand of Converse knockoffs, called *Buddies*. My mom did not understand that sending me to school in Buddies was like giving a starving dog a rubber bone. Buddies were not just a poor substitute; they were an open invitation to ridicule, scorn, and abuse. By virtue of our diminished footwear status, those of us caught wearing Buddies were always emotionally and, many times, physically brutalized.

Being beaten and beaten down because your family could not afford a certain kind of shoe was the apotheosis of adding insult to injury. It was also as patently absurd as it was humiliating because, from a distance, Kmart Buddy shoes looked almost exactly like authentic Converse Chuck Taylors. You had to get close to see the differences. But in the cutthroat social realm that was high school, there were kids who made it their business to discern who had the real goods and who had the frauds—who, in other words, were the pretenders.

So, starting from below my ankles with discount footwear, I learned at a young age about the dangers of letting people get too close. If I could keep people at a distance, I would look like everyone else. But I knew if they got close enough, they'd be able to see the real me, a fraud, play-acting to be anything but what I actually was: an emotionally unstable teenager barely hanging on and a desperate amalgamation of insecurities and doubts who was running out of excuses to keep his misery going for even another day, another hour.

I was, in other words, exactly the sort of person for whom alcohol and drugs would provide relief and release. If I could get out of my own skin, I could stop feeling, and if I could stop feeling, I could make it through the day.

Mine was one of millions of such stories. Psychoactive drugs creating euphoria in a young mind and body that knows only pain and disappointment, predictably, transform from the solution, to a medium-size problem, into a giant-size, life-threatening problem of its own.

I was taught how to drink alcohol at an early age, and it was the easiest substance to get. I was a regular drinker during high school and quickly incorporated weed and, on occasion, other people's prescription pills.

Predictably, my years of high school were mostly a disaster, and I dropped out, a year short of graduation. With no responsibilities, I mostly drank and used drugs.

By the time I was 20 years old, my self-image was sufficiently diminished that I thought I would be lucky if I could ever obtain and hold on to a menial job and somehow live independently. I was a high school dropout with no real skills, few good options, and dim prospects.

In those years, drinking and getting high were vitally important parts of my day. Being without the means to get high was unthinkable. It was worse than no food in the fridge or no gas in the car. In fact, when necessity required me to choose between life's essentials, on more than a few occasions, the gas tank and the refrigerator went unfilled so I could buy alcohol.

So, if for no other reason than to maintain my daily escape, I had to earn some money. And since crime was probably out of the question because I considered myself too limited to mastermind anything without getting caught, I needed to find a job, any job, even a lousy job.

I applied for and eagerly accepted a position that fit my self-image to a tee. At the age of about 22, I became a garbage man, and if it were possible to hate anything more than I already hated myself, I'd found it: I despised that job.

But I halted my substance use for long enough to get through my probationary period, and then I resumed drinking, getting high, showing up late, and missing work.

After one particularly egregious offense, I was presented with an ultimatum: I could either go to our company's employee assistance program (EAP) or I could be terminated on the spot.

So I went to the EAP—which was little more than a few dingy offices in the basement of an old house—and saw a guy named Ron, who asked me why I was there, and, before I answered, said, "Before you begin to answer you should know this: I've been to prison eight times and a dope fiend my whole life. I have been around criminals, drug addicts, and alcoholics since I was 5 years old. This is your opportunity to be honest with me. But, whatever you do, please do not try to bullshit a bullshitter."

He proceeded to interrogate me, and, for perhaps the first time in my adult life, I told the truth. No sense trying to bullshit a bullshitter, I thought. So, I admitted that a number of things in my life were not exactly going swimmingly; I told him how much I'd been drinking and misusing drugs—I even told him that I'd been thinking of killing myself.

And it was with that admission—in that dim, dank basement, to a man who was, for all intents and purposes, a total stranger—that something shifted, and I had a moment of clarity. For the first time I knew I was sick. I knew I felt bad. And I knew I wanted to feel better.

At Ron's urging and under his supervision, I walked into an addiction treatment clinic where I began the long journey to sobriety and recovery. I was there for about a month, and Ron stayed with me during my stay and long after my discharge.

There was almost nothing about treatment with Ron—who, as he admitted, was an ex-con with few formal credentials but a PhD from the school of hard knocks—or the staff of the treatment center, that was readily identified as "evidenced based." But by the time a month had passed, I experienced a transformational, tectonic shift in my thinking, my ability to feel, and my will and desire to go on living.

Arguably, the single most potent ingredient of my time with Ron was not any one thing he said, but rather was my connection to Ron's gut instincts about how to create a relationship with me in which change could occur.

In other words, Ron built a *therapeutic alliance* with me. Without this, nothing would have changed. But *with it*, almost anything was possible.

Building a therapeutic alliance quickly is a key to the likely success or failure of any approach to treatment. While becoming a professional counselor involves learning a number of quantifiable and teachable clinical skills, knowing how to build a therapeutic alliance and making it happen within the first hour is both art and science. Ron, my untrained counselor with little formal education sensed how to build that bridge. He threw me a lifeline and, for reasons I still don't entirely understand, I grabbed it.

In retrospect, it's clear that Ron's clinical toolbox was small, and it was undoubtedly insufficient for every person he encountered. All he knew was how to be himself and how to administer brutal honesty with genuine empathy. And while authenticity is essential, scientists really don't know how to categorize a guy like Ron. They call him an "*n* of 1," an outlier. Meaning he, as a unique person with idiosyncratic techniques, *is* the intervention. But for me, also an *n* of 1, it worked.

With little more than those two skills, he taught me how to have a life without alcohol and drugs. He taught me how to live one day at a time and take on problems in the same manner. Whenever I got stuck or discouraged, he knew what to say and how to say it—at least what to say and how to say it *to me*.

The addiction treatment I received in 1989 was nothing special, and, in fact, my outcome was the exception. I got well while most of the people who entered the program with me dropped out. There were few happy endings among our cohort. The success rate then, as now, was abysmally poor.

Now, fast forward three decades, and the only real advances between my treatment and the treatment offered today might include a new medication or two or a greater understanding that addiction is a brain disease. But the alarming truth is that the systems and practices within the walls of treatment centers today are, for the most part, the same as they were 30, 40, even 50 years ago.

Then, as now, addiction treatment is little more than a schedule of activities that seem like they might be helpful but are not evidence based.

For example, my treatment started with a morning meditation and then breakfast. Then we had maybe group therapy, "chalk talk" (educational lectures), art therapy, physical activities in the basketball gym or tennis court, individual counseling sessions that were mostly chitchat about our willingness to continue in the program, and lots and lots of breaks.

An hour before dinner was devoted to book time. We sat in a classroom and would take turns reading out of a book, *Alcoholics Anonymous: The Story of How Many Thousands of Men and Women Have Recovered From Alcoholism*.

It was written in 1939, mostly by Bill Wilson, one of the founders of Alcoholics Anonymous (AA). Better known as AA's *Big Book* (because the first edition was printed on very thick paper), it's gone on to become one of the bestselling books in history. It is no one's definition a medical or scientific book, but just as it had been for addiction sufferers in the 1940s and 1950s, it served as our road atlas to recovery. It is still in use today.

I've been clean and sober for over 30 years. My recovery was facilitated by methods that, to a large extent, were neither evidence based nor even likely to succeed. I got damn lucky, and to this day I carry with me a boatload of gratitude for my good fortune.

Addiction was my first big problem, and, against long odds, I recovered. My second big problem began with a garden-variety headache.

As a person who's made it to the ripe old age of 57 without any other major health concerns, I'm not accustomed to aches and pains. So on those rare occasions when something hurts, I generally do nothing and wait until it goes away.

Earlier in 2020 I didn't think much about a nettlesome headache—until I was entering my second week of it. And when I could no longer deny that I had a constant, throbbing pain in my skull that was undiminished by the Tylenol I was throwing at it every 4 hours, I figured I should probably see someone.

But the COVID-19 pandemic was straining hospital capacity. I had no desire to expose myself to the coronavirus or take up space in an emergency room for something as trivial as a headache, well, a headache and some intermittent dizziness.

I called a primary care doctor, and, after I described all of my symptoms to him, he was concerned enough to send me for a computed tomographic, or CT scan—and that got my attention.

Over the next several days, my symptoms worsened. It felt as if a sadistic dentist was running a drill into the back of my eyes—that was worrisome.

Soon I was talking to a neurosurgeon, and 24 hours after that I was lying in a magnetic resonance imaging tube listening to a cacophony of metallic clanging as the machine built an image, layer by layer, of what was inside my head.

The phone call from the doctor came later that afternoon. He told me I had a grape size lesion on my brain. It resided near the back of my head, on the right side. He went on to say that it had an odd, irregular, asymmetrical shape. As he let that sink in, he added, "You know what we're looking at here, don't you David?"

I guess he didn't want to tell me I had brain cancer, so he made me say it. And when I did, he validated the conclusion and said, "We need to get that tumor out of your head right away."

My wife was beside me when I put the phone down. She held me, and, surrendering to the uncertainty and fear, we both cried.

After 4 more days of vertigo, nausea, and blinding headaches, the time of my craniotomy arrived. I awoke early and showered with a special antibacterial soap and shampoo. I was transferred to the anesthesia area and, from there, the operating theater.

I was positioned face down with my head pinned to the table. My neurosurgeon made a 6-inch incision in my scalp, then spread it apart in order to remove a section of my skull. Using a laser and blades specially developed for this purpose, the tumor was carefully excised.

Once it was removed, my head was scanned again with magnetic resonance imaging to check for any missed lesions.

When he determined that he'd removed all he could, he replaced the section of my skull and stitched my scalp back together.

Forty-eight hours later, I was home. My headaches, dizziness, and vision problems were gone, and, all things considered, I felt pretty good.

Unfortunately, my biopsy came back with some bad news: *Grade 4 glioblastoma wild type.* The neurosurgeon strongly urged me not to google this diagnosis. I knew enough to follow his advice and didn't search for more information. That was about 5 months ago, and there's still a lot I don't know.

I have entrusted my fate to the team of experts in neurosurgery and oncology at the Alvin J. Siteman Center for Advanced Medicine at Washington University in St. Louis, Missouri. I know my disease is serious and not fully understood, but I believe in science, and there are few places in the world where I might receive better care.

I can't help but to contrast my treatment for this serious brain disease with the treatment of addiction, my other serious brain disease.

Many of the physicians providing my cancer treatment have both an MD (with 5–7 years of radiology and oncology training after medical school) and a PhD from a leading research university. They have all seen hundreds of other patients with my diagnosis, their knowledge is current, and they employ the best evidence-based practices. Their nurses, physician assistants, and other staff members are sensitive, warm, and, inasmuch as circumstances permit, reassuring. Everyone appears to be committed to doing everything in their considerable power to improve my odds and buy me many good years.

My addiction therapist was a high school graduate, and his primary qualification was his own recovery from the disease.

There is an established treatment regime for my cancer that uses both radiation and chemotherapy. Its treatment has a sequence of events that leads to a conclusion and is closely and regularly monitored.

I take a drug (Temodar) specifically designed to shrink glioblastomas in a prescribed dose (160 mg/day for 42 days). One hour before taking the Temodar, I take another pill to reduce nausea. I endure radiation every day for the same 6 weeks, and I'm instructed to take my pill 1 hour before the radiation is focused on my brain. Research has shown that using chemotherapy concurrently with radiation works better than using them consecutively.

After 6 weeks, my dose of Temodar is doubled on 5 days each month for the next 6 months, and during this 6-month phase, I will wear a special headgear called *Optune* for at least 18 hours per day. It's a portable, device approved by the Food and Drug Administration that looks like a wiring harness attached to a swim cap. Optune generates low-intensity electric fields that interfere with glioblastoma tumor cell division. These electric fields slow or stop the tumor cells from dividing and may help destroy them— all good things. According to the data, 43 percent of people using Optune while receiving chemotherapy were alive at 2 years compared to only 31 percent of people on chemo alone. Wearing this device 18 hours a day might sound like a hardship, but if it gives me extra months, it's a small price to pay. Treatment for cancer involves surgery, radiation, and drugs. All have been studied extensively in randomized, controlled studies. Surgical techniques are standardized and delivered with checklists so no steps are skipped or misordered. Drugs are prescribed in specific dosages. Radiation is measured precisely. Everyone is treated according to established protocols. All treatment outcomes are tracked and quantified.

Today's treatment for addiction could not be more different. It's not even treatment; it's just a schedule of daily activities that gets repeated over and over again without much of any new information. No wonder outcomes are either poor or, more typically, hidden or unknown.

I believe in science, and I trust in data. So far, the medical team at Washington University has demonstrated great familiarity with the treatment of my disease. They know what to measure during regular laboratory tests and office visits, and they study the results carefully. There are few opinions, but there are many facts. The facts, and the science, guide my treatment, not anyone's gut feelings about what might be helpful.

I recovered from addiction despite unproven treatment from mostly untrained providers. My recovery from this second brain disease, despite proven treatment from the most highly trained providers in the world, remains uncertain.

Substance use disorder was my first big problem, and I recovered from it. I am fighting my current illness as I make the final edits of this book, trying to ensure it will be worthy of publication. To a great extent, I am writing this book because successful outcomes in the addiction field should not be as rare or unusual as mine was. They should be *routine*. And they can be made routine if only we approach this cunning disease with the same fervor with which science, data, and technologies attack other cunning diseases.

Like brain cancer.

Editor's Note

David Patterson began writing this book at the end of 2019. By the time he completed the manuscript in early summer, 2020, two extraordinary and unfortunate things had taken place. David mentions both in the pages that follow, but the reader might find his observations to be frustratingly incomplete.

First, and most obviously, David wrote the majority of the book right before and during the early stages of the COVID-19 pandemic. The world had only begun to fall off its axis, and in the first half of 2020, there was no way to predict just how long and how much this was going to affect the United States and the rest of the world.

But in addition to the disease caused by a novel coronavirus that disrupted life on earth, David mentions in this book that he was diagnosed with another, very serious illness in 2020 . . . and then he goes on to address other subjects and never offers the reader an update on his condition.

As he writes in the introduction to this book, David was afflicted with a terrible and virulent brain cancer. Though he almost certainly knew it when his doctor gave him the news, he did not write that his condition was terminal. Both he and his wife, Nikki, stayed positive and hopeful throughout the months of difficult radiation and chemotherapy, and though David grew increasingly impaired, he never complained or bemoaned his fate. In the end, the glioblastoma did what it almost always does, and it ended David's life way too soon.

This is why some of the ideas and innovations expressed in this book are fully formed but not fully finished. It will be up to readers like you to take the hints, the clues, and the crystal-clear directions that David provides, and make real the vision he lays out for you.

We would like to close this note by adding a final word of thanks, to expand a bit on the acknowledgments section that the author wrote as his health was failing. It is not a stretch to say that this book would not have been finished without the help of Howard Weissman, a friend and colleague of David's, who stepped in to assist with the final stages of production to ensure that David's voice and message carried through, while attending to necessary edits and corrections. Finally, to David—we are grateful for the chance to have known you and remain in awe of your courage and determination to see this book through even as you knew you might not ever hold it in your hands. David A. Patterson Silver Wolf, passed away on May 14, 2021.

Introduction

At 2:15 p.m. on the afternoon of January 13, 1982, Air Florida Flight 90, a Boeing 737-222, was scheduled to fly from Washington, D.C., to Fort Lauderdale, with an intermediate stop in Tampa. Seventy-four passengers and a crew of four people were on board.

The weather was bad in our nation's capital that day. So much snow (more than 6 inches) had been falling that Washington (now called Reagan) National Airport shut down for more than an hour to give maintenance crews time to clear the runways. This had affected all afternoon flights scheduled to leave D.C., including Flight 90, which was delayed 1 hour and 45 minutes. While the Boeing 737 sat on the ground waiting to head off to Florida, falling snow continued to stick to its wings and fuselage.

During the delay, Flight 90 and all other planes scheduled for departure were de-iced. Whenever snow or ice has accumulated on an aircraft, the pilots call on the airport de-icing facility to spray the plane with a heated mixture of a glycol and water to remove it. When the airport reopened at 2:53 p.m., the crew on Flight 90 requested the de-icing to commence, and the airport deployed a team to do the job. It took quite a while to cover all of the large plane's flight control surfaces with the fluid, and by the time the de-icing was finished, the flight crew still had to contend with the 2 to 3 inches of new snow that had accumulated on the ground around the idling plane. There was enough snow on the ground that the motorized tug (the small vehicle that pushes the plane away from the gate) was unable to budge the aircraft, so the pilot, impatient to get on his way, started the engines at the gate and applied reverse thrust in an attempt to help the tug. Though the pilot probably already knew it, the tug operator cautioned him that this maneuver was against company policy. Worse, it didn't free the plane.

The engines only ran for a minute or so in this stationary position, but they managed to blow a significant amount of snow off the ground and out of the engines, back over the recently de-iced plane. Then, approximately 40 minutes after the reopening of the airport and the initial de-icing of Flight 90, a second tug, this one better equipped for the weather, was brought to

The New Addiction Treatment. David A. Patterson Silver Wolf, Oxford University Press. © Oxford University Press 2021.
DOI: 10.1093/oso/9780197601372.003.0001

the gate and required 6 minutes to successfully push the snow-covered plane away from the terminal, where Flight 90 then motored under its own power onto the taxiway with both its engines running.

Every commercial airplane contains an automatic cockpit voice recorder to capture everything that is said or heard during a flight, and the recording begins just before the aircraft pushes away from the gate. Passenger airline protocols require the captain to go through a post–engine start checklist on every flight, and indeed, the cockpit voice recorder on Flight 90 captured the captain going through his checklist. Nothing out of the ordinary was indicated, though he was heard to say that the anti-ice function of the plane was turned off at 2:46 p.m. (7 minutes after being put in the taxi lineup and 53 minutes after the de-icing). During the checklist conversation with the copilot, both men commented on the half-inch or so of ice visible on the wings of the plane. The captain did not seem overly concerned, stating only the inside of the wing needed to be clean, and the speed they would fly at would "shuck all the other stuff off." Later in the same conversation, the first officer declared that de-icing the wings was a "losing battle" and all de-icing did was give a "false feeling of security." This may explain why the pilots failed to switch on the engines' internal ice protection systems.

The captain, Larry Wheaton, was 34 years old and had about 8,300 total flight hours, including 1,752 hours on the Boeing 737. The first officer, Roger Pettit, a former U.S. Air Force fighter jock, was 31, with approximately 3,353 total flight hours. Both men had done most of their flying in Florida and other warm weather climates.

This may explain their reasoning and the opinions (i.e., practice wisdom) about the limited value of de-icing the plane and their unconcern about the conditions.

With ice on the wings and snow covering the plane, the aircraft was cleared for departure without a second de-icing.

It went bad immediately.

Right from the start, first officer Pettit indicated that something did not seem right. He repeated this observation two more times. But at no point did Captain Wheaton decide to abort their takeoff.

As the plane barreled down the runway, Pettit can be heard saying, "God, look at that thing. That don't seem right, does it? Uh, that's not right."

Captain Wheaton, clearly focused on his increasing speed, readying himself to pull back on the yoke and take the lumbering jet airborne, dismisses this, saying "Yes, it is. There's 80 [referring to knots, their speed on the runway]."

First officer Pettit is not reassured and says "Naw, I don't think that's right." Then, as if trying to convince himself, says, "Maybe it is."

Captain Larry Wheaton announces: "Hundred and twenty" and cockpit sounds indicate that he's pulling back on the stick, trying to get the heavy jet in the air, but there isn't enough lift.

The two men can be heard trying to coax the plane higher. "Forward, forward, easy. We only want 500 [feet]."

"Come on forward . . . forward, just barely climb," the captain urges.

But the aircraft will not obey. One of the men, panic rising in his voice, says, "Stalling, we're falling!"

The sounds of the stick shaker can be heard, along with horns and alarms. Then, at 4:01 p.m., Roger Pettit utters his last words: "Larry," he says to his captain, "We're going down, Larry."

Captain Larry Wheaton's final three words are, "I know it."

The plane struck the 14th Street Bridge, a few blocks from the White House. It broke apart and plunged into the Potomac River. Seventy passengers and four crew members, including the pilot and first officer, were killed, along with four people driving across the bridge at the moment of impact. There were four survivors.

The following investigation revealed a number of troubling pilot errors. It was learned that 2 years before the crash, Captain Wheaton had been suspended due to not adhering to regulations, failing to conduct standard flight checklists, and failing to follow flight protocols during departures. Three months later, he passed a test and was fully reinstated. Just 8 months after that, he again received unsatisfactory scores on a written exam on issues related to such things as aircraft limitations. However, just a few days later, a retest showed proficiency in those areas. And 8 months after that, Captain Wheaton settled into the cockpit of Flight 90.

Seventy-four souls lost their lives on that afternoon because the professionals in charge of Flight 90 deviated from established, proven procedures and instead trusted their gut, their own personal experience.

Had the flight crew lived, they would have been held to account for their decisions. They were blamed in death, but so too was the airline, the aircraft manufacturer, the airport, and everyone who had any role—real or imagined—in not successfully and safely conveying passengers from Washington to Florida.

It is easy to understand the anger and legal consequences that arise when airline pilots deviate from accepted, proven procedures.

What is less well known but equally egregious is what happens when a person in the throes of an active addiction puts their faith and their fate in the hands of a person or place that deviates from evidence-based methods or operates on intuition. The outcome can be similarly disastrous, but the response is wholly different.

When addiction treatment fails, the only person blamed, the only person held to account, and the only person to suffer negative consequences is the person who sought help: the patient.

In addiction treatment—just like in commercial air travel—a professional is employed to take an individual from one place to another. In both cases, lives are on the line.

While there is no written airline contract that guarantees a successful trip, the flying public does have the expectation that pilots are well trained and employing the safest and most proven technologies and professional practices.

We hold similar expectations of our surgeons and physicians. We do not expect eternal life and health, but we do expect our healthcare professionals to deliver proven, evidence-based treatment. We also expect that they measure and monitor their performance so that when certain practices or procedures generate poor outcomes, those activities are changed. And if they don't follow those practices and procedures, when things go badly they are held responsible and they suffer consequences for the harm they have caused.

It seems reasonable then, that addiction treatment facilities should be held to a similar standard. Yet today, amid the worst drug epidemic in modern American history, our addiction treatment industry does not hold itself or its practitioners responsible for delivering proven, evidence-based treatment or achieving even modestly successful outcomes. This industry does not use any kind of real-time, data-guided services to inform its system. It is based on old assumptions and ideas that were established over 70 years ago. When failure occurs, it is always—and only—the fault of the patient.

Tens of thousands of Americans die prematurely from various addictions each year.[1] About 20 million Americans seek treatment for their addiction-related problems annually, and that number could double as more people gain access to insurance and services through the Affordable Care Act.[2] In spite of so many needing help, very few of these people will receive coordinated professional services based on treatment methods scientifically proven to work.[3]

When we go to the doctor, we expect to receive evidence-based medicine. This is not so much the gold standard as it is the minimum standard. Yet strict adherence to evidence-based interventions or performance-based practices is neither required of nor delivered in the treatment of addictions.

The National Institute of Drug Abuse's report, *Adoption of NIDA's Evidence-Based Treatments in Real World Settings*,[4] indicated that the addiction treatment field must more consistently find ways to implement *existing interventions* in real-world settings.

According to NIDA's report, the problem is not a lack of proven interventions—there exist several that are both effective and evidence-based—it is the infrequency with which they are actually delivered.

In other words, the NIDA report concluded that there is little need to develop and test additional behavioral interventions at this point. Until the interventions we already know to work are put into real-world practice, developing *new* evidence-based methods or techniques is a waste of valuable time and diminishing resources. Our primary effort, or so it seems to me, should be the vigorous and rigorous deployment of the data-driven, evidence-based treatment methods that already exist, along with being ready, willing, and able to incorporate new, technological tools that support long-term, sustained recovery.

The idea for this book began with a simple, but troubling, question: Who in the addiction treatment industry (e.g., researchers, educators, treatment organizations, frontline therapists, etc.) has the moral obligation to ensure that evidence-based interventions are used in addiction services and that patients are receiving high-quality, effective services that are supported by data?

There are many reasons why the continued use of evidence-based methods has not found its way to addiction treatment, and we explore them in later chapters.

But for now, let me reveal my personal bias and say this: If we are to materially improve addiction treatment outcomes and bring science to service, we need to first ask questions that are grounded in *morality*, not science.

For instance, we must ask *who* is ultimately responsible for ensuring that patients receive only those services that have been validated by scientific evidence. Most, if not all, research questions ask *why* rather than *who*.

Asking and answering the important question of *who is responsible* for providing quality addiction care might help resolve one of the central dilemmas in the treatment of this deadly illness: Is addiction a disease, or is it a personal failing? Any enlightened person and exactly every single provider of addiction services would stridently argue that it is, of course, a disease.

But it remains the only disease that, when unsuccessfully treated, becomes the failure of the patient. Even today, the best and the brightest minds who are quick to describe addiction as a chronic brain disease are equally quick to use phrases like, "She wasn't ready for treatment," or "He just couldn't leave his old life and start a new one."

Is it any wonder, then, that the stigma and misunderstanding surrounding this particular disease persists? Is it any wonder why public figures have been heard voicing the opinion that rising overdose death rates serve to "cull the herd"? Is it any wonder why this illness receives a fraction of the attention and funding afforded other chronic diseases, even while it exacts a far higher price on our social and economic fabrics?

Breathtakingly high failure rates have become acceptable through the treatment system. Our profession has had a preposterously long run of not being held accountable for its patients' care. I believe that run must end.

To accomplish this, the entire system needs to be called into question. Because, simply stated, if the treatment delivery system does not benefit the people it seeks to serve, it must be re-formed.

When an airplane crashes, an investigative team searches for defects in the aircraft and tries to understand what the pilots did or did not do. This is an effort to seek the truth, to understand the exact nature of the problem so no one else will suffer a similar fatal, an avoidable crash. When a patient fails in treatment, the usual protocol is to search the *patient* for defects.

Professional workers quickly target the patient's shortcomings while advocating for more resources to solve the patient's problems. At no point does anyone listen to the *cockpit voice recorder* or examine the *black box* in order to understand the failure. There are few *internal systems flaw* investigations conducted or mandated *root cause analyses* throughout the treatment industry.

One of the reasons I am comparing addiction treatment with air travel is because both are in the business of "transporting" people from Point A to Point B. For anyone who has booked a flight lately, you know almost everything is accomplished remotely, using technology. You can use a search engine or third-party travel service to explore and evaluate different service providers, compare what each flight would cost, its flight path, number of layovers, what seats are open, and so on.

A customer can select which options are best for their travel. The customer can also see reviews and other information, such as how often that particular flight runs late.

The 900 million customers entering the airline services each year have a fair amount of information and insights into the flying experience. They understand the process of getting from Point A to Point B, and while they may not know the statistics (there is about a 1 in 5 million chance of experiencing a fatal plane crash, which is a 0.00002 percent chance of dying), they know commercial airline travel is safe.

While it is likely that the plane will land safely, it will also arrive at its intended destination. While not guaranteed, airlines will get their passengers and their luggage to the right airport in the right city about 95 percent of the time.

Imagine you helped get your loved one onto a flight that was to arrive in Albuquerque, New Mexico. When you discovered she ended up in St. Louis, Missouri, you ask an airline worker what happened. He responds: "Well, we believed your mom just wasn't ready to arrive in Albuquerque yet."

This would be unacceptable in the airline industry, and most likely if an organization operated using these tactics, it would soon have no customers to blame.

Patients receiving addiction treatment are receiving all the blame for that treatment's failure when they should be offered the same respect and sympathy given to those who did not arrive at their planned destinations. Just as when the outcome is disastrous for an airline flight, if patients do not make it safely to their planned destinations, their loved ones should be assured that lessons were learned, policies and procedures were changed, and the odds of another failure have been reduced.

The treatment industry must find its moral footing and rebuild its structures to achieve better and more acceptable outcomes. If front-line therapists and treatment organizations are held accountable for their patients' care, the way we educate and train professional staff will change, the methods and questions we research will change, our community-based social services will change, and our patients will finally be provided with the *performance-based, science-based services* they so very much deserve.

This book is a humble attempt to initiate a shift to heightened accountability and measured performance. Our system and its workers can no longer be allowed to provide services based on old practices, hunches, and assumptions. We have the scientific knowledge and technological capabilities to provide front-line therapists with the tools necessary to decrease the failure rate in our system, and this industry should be *forced*, if necessary, to use them. Knowing that change by force is often unsuccessful and unwise, the best way to ensure change is by disrupting this industry with a new, modernized system of care.

Treatment providers and the structures that feed and fund them, along with our education, training, and research systems, will all soon have to decide whether they continue with their yellow cab enterprise or enter into the new world of Uber.

In the effort to discuss the new and improved approaches of treatment, this book contains three parts. The first part looks at the size and scope of the problem, examining why patients are not receiving services based on science and enumerating the other issues that lead to poor outcomes for addiction treatment. The second part discusses possible solutions to these problems. The third part offers a vision of how addiction treatment services should and it is hoped will be conducted in the near future.

My objective is to bring attention to a long-neglected issue and perhaps disrupt this industry's practices by questioning some of its most deeply rooted beliefs and values and providing a rationale for moving to a higher standard of care.

It should be noted that I sometimes use the most commonly understood term, *addiction*, when discussing the illness. The proper medical term is *substance use disorder*. However, in some sentences, use of the three-word phrase can be cumbersome. So, *addiction* and *substance use disorder* are used interchangeably. I do not wish to use any stigmatizing language or labels, so words or phrases with negative connotations, like *addict* or *substance abuser* have been eschewed.

PART I
THE PROBLEM

1

How Big Is Big?

There is no one who doubts that alcohol and other drugs create enormous—and enormously expensive—problems worldwide and here in the United States.

Much of the media coverage in local and national news has focused on the opioid epidemic, and rightly so. Opioids are highly addictive and often lethal. And at the peak of the epidemic, in 2017, overdose deaths *from opioids alone*, climbed to about 47,000 per year, an astounding number.[5,6]

More astounding is that same year (and the year before and the year after) nearly twice as many were killed by alcohol.

Problems related to the consumption of alcoholic beverages result in about 88,000 premature deaths annually, approximately 62,000 men and 26,000 women.[7] According to the National Institute of Alcohol Abuse and Alcoholism, alcohol is the third leading contributor to mortality related to lifestyle in the United States (after tobacco use and diet/activity patterns).

There are various theories about why alcohol continues to kill so many more people than do opioids without setting off public health alarms, but the prevailing view is, at its essence, one of hopeless resignation.

Alcohol has been around since biblical days and is intertwined in our culture and religious belief systems. Both secular and religious rites and rituals are almost always accompanied by alcohol. From the four glasses of wine at a Jewish Seder, to the popping of champagne corks on New Year's Eve, to the toasts at a wedding, or to the raised glasses at a wake, alcohol has become inextricably bound with the way we worship, the way we celebrate, and the way we grieve.

With worldwide sales in excess of $1 trillion,[8] alcohol isn't going anywhere. And based on the near utter disinterest for funding comprehensive, pervasive prevention education initiatives, the incidence of fetal alcohol spectrum disorders (the leading preventable birth defect in the United States, affecting 1 out of 100 babies—more than Down syndrome, cerebral palsy, sudden infant death syndrome, cystic fibrosis, and spina bifida combined), the number

The New Addiction Treatment. David A. Patterson Silver Wolf, Oxford University Press. © Oxford University Press 2021. DOI: 10.1093/oso/9780197601372.003.0002

of alcohol-related deaths and the already-exorbitant social costs are unlikely to decrease any time soon.

While the costs related to human suffering are enormous and, to a large extent, incalculable, the economic costs *can* be estimated, but they are no less astounding. In 2010, alcohol misuse cost the United States $249 billion, or about $1,000 for every American over the age of 18.

And that's just alcohol; when drugs (both legal and illicit) are included, the United States spends more than $820 billion annually on substance abuse and addiction.[9] That is considerably more than the amount allocated for our entire national defense budget.

And this is merely the financial toll (e.g., lost productivity, healthcare costs, law enforcement, etc.) depicted on a chart many will skim over (Appendix A). Our minds get numb when we hear or read about figures in the hundreds of millions, let alone the billions. Numbers like these are impersonal; they are abstractions.

The only number that matters is one. The one person you loved who was lost to active addiction or death—the one child, the one parent, the one sibling . . .

And we all have one. Or we all know one. Or we all know *of* one. Or, more likely, we all know of more than one. There are millions of those ones being lost to a disease for which there is life-saving and life-changing treatment, but only a tiny fraction of the ones we know, the ones we love—only one out of many—will find the right help and find their way to recovery.

New guidelines define alcohol use disorder as a chronic relapsing brain disease characterized by compulsive alcohol use, loss of control over alcohol intake, and increased negative emotions when not using alcohol.[10] This broader definition should not be taken lightly.

There does seem to be a genetic predisposition to alcohol use disorder, so, of course, it is a condition, like balding or breast cancer, that tends to run in the family. However, just because a genetic predisposition exists does not mean it manifests. A 2008 study estimated that genetic factors account for roughly 40-60 percent of the variance in those with alcohol use disorders.[11]

Therefore, it is nurture as well as nature. Family environment and personal choice make a huge difference between who will and who will not develop problems later in life. Studies have shown children who grow up witnessing problem alcohol use are more likely to develop abuse problems when they get older. Considering that more than 10 percent of U.S. children live under the same roof as at least one parent with an alcohol problem,[12] many millions of today's children are likely to develop drinking problems of their own.

The example set by parents with their own drinking has been shown to affect their children's drinking throughout their lifetime.[13] How often parents consume alcohol, how much they consume at each sitting, the situations and contexts in which parents use alcohol, and their attitudes and expectations about alcohol use are all routes by which young people's patterns of behavior can be formed long before they begin making their own decisions about drinking. Other elements of the family structure, and how the child responds to it, can also influence a child's behavior. These include things like parenting style; the level of attachment and bonding between parent and child; the level of nurturance, abuse, or neglect; and the presence or absence of discipline and monitoring. Problem drinking, in other words, often starts many years before kids actually begin consuming alcohol.

And what is *problem* drinking? Do we rate it or give it a grade?

Today, there are generally three coded categories of alcohol use:

Current users are people who have had at least one drink in the past month.

Binge users have had at least four or five drinks on the same occasion in the past month.

Heavy users have had at least four to five drinks on the same occasion on at least five different days in the past month.[14]

So, while all heavy use drinkers are binge drinkers, not all binge drinkers are heavy users.

Moreover, by definition, problems only arise after a person becomes a current user.

Of concern is the number of teens and preteens who cross over into current use. It is not a legal or moral judgment that anyone under the age of 21 should not consume alcohol; it is the peril young people face when consuming a dangerous, addictive substance long before their brains have fully developed. The teen brain is growing and making connections at a furious rate. Just as a teenager can take up the guitar or master French faster than an adult, that same neural plasticity makes them more vulnerable to "learn how" to become addicted.

While numbers have been falling since the 2002 survey, the Substance Abuse and Mental Health Services Administration's 2015 National Survey on Drug Use and Health reported about one of every five (roughly 20.3 percent)

Americans aged 12 years or older consumed alcohol in the past month.[15] That means nearly eight million kids are drinking alcohol on a regular basis. Worse, roughly two thirds of them reported binge drinking, and 1.3 million classified themselves as heavy alcohol users. Despite numbers like these, almost no federal monies are allocated for prevention education—a set of evidence-based interventions that, when properly administered, could lead to a dramatic increase in the number of kids postponing the age at which they initiate alcohol use.

According to the 2016 National Survey on Drug Use and Health, 51 percent of Americans are current drinkers; close behind, 48 percent are binge drinkers, and 12 percent will meet the criteria for heavy use.

In other words, almost eighteen million U.S. adults are currently wrestling with an active, diagnosable, full-fledged alcohol use disorder, and less than 8 percent of those will receive treatment.[16]

While alcohol is usually studied separately from other addictive substances, many people struggling with alcohol use disorder also use other mood- or mind-altering substances. Said differently, describing the incidence, prevalence, and costs associated with the misuse of alcohol is but the tip of the iceberg. The national appetite to get high is not limited to beer, wine, and spirits. Other drugs, both licit and illicit, add to our national addiction woes.

In this country, nearly 10 percent of all individuals over the age of 11 are engaged in some form of illicit drug use, which includes the use of otherwise legal prescription medications used for nonmedical purposes.[12]

Unsurprisingly, marijuana was the most commonly reported drug, with nearly twenty million users. This is a number that is sure to climb as marijuana use is increasingly normalized, legalized, and, inevitably, commercialized.

Alcohol and drug use trends

The National Survey on Drug Use and Health, which interviews around 70,000 people (or about seventy times more than the number interviewed for the average political poll) aged 12 and older about drug and alcohol use, points to the following trends: In 1979, of the population aged 12 and older, 14 percent reported using an illicit drug in the past 30 days. From 1979 to 1999, this number steadily fell to a low of 6 percent in 1999, thanks in part to greater education efforts and changes in cultural attitudes.

But between 1999 and 2001, use again began to increase, and by 2013, surveys revealed that roughly twenty-five million Americans (9 percent of those over 12 years old) had used an illicit drug within the past month. This bump, according to the National Institute on Drug Abuse, was largely attributable to the changing status of cannabis. As the use of other drugs (with the exception of methamphetamine) have stabilized or declined, cannabis use is ascendant (Appendix B).

The bottom line

It was estimated that in 2017, about twenty million Americans, or fully 10 percent of everyone above the age of 12, met the diagnostic criteria for a substance use disorder. This is the number who could benefit from professional treatment services. And of those twenty million people needing treatment, only 1.4 percent actually received any treatment for their disorder.

The numbers haven't changed that much, so right now, in America, there are about sixteen million people mingling among us, teaching our children, serving our food, driving our Ubers and our school buses, arresting and judging and operating on us, who are themselves sufficiently affected by alcohol and/or drugs that they need—and are not receiving—medically supervised detox and long-term rehabilitative services.

Further, on top of the sixteen million Americans who need treatment, there are another eighty-two million, though not quite drinking enough alcohol to merit an alcohol use disorder diagnosis, who are drinking more than enough to do themselves harm and put themselves at high risk of developing a host of medical problems.

We are, in other words, a country awash in the disease of addiction, and it is a condition we are passing on to our children.

At the risk of sounding Cassandra-like, this poses an existential threat to our way of life and, not unlike climate change, our civilization. If we do not find a way to slow or stop the rate of substance-induced death and destruction, we may be careening toward an impoverished, dystopian future.

2

Failure Is an Option

Rosa Esparza was not a small woman. On the night of July 19, 2013, the 52-year-old mother and grandmother had a little trouble squeezing into the Texas Giant roller coaster seat.[17] Her daughter and son-in-law jumped the car ahead of her, and it took Rosa some extra time to ease herself into the car behind them. Though the seats were uncomfortable, Rosa enjoyed the thrill of roller coasters, and, as was her first visit to Arlington's Six Flags Over Texas, she looked forward to riding all of them.

In the boarding area, a Six Flags employee noticed that Rosa's lap bar did not appear to be properly secured. Though the park had a clear "if-in-doubt" safety policy that empowered employees to stop the ride if they had the slightest concern, this young man allowed the train to proceed. Though the T-bar was the only means of holding passengers in their cars, more than 2.5 million riders preceded Rosa on this ride without a mishap; surely, this was not the first time someone rode without the bar locked down tight.

The Texas Giant roller coaster ascended more than 14 stories before rocketing down its curvy tracks at breakneck speeds.

Rosa Esparza had trouble right away. As the train made its climb, Rosa's daughter, sitting one car ahead, turned, horrified, to see her mom turned nearly upside down. As the coaster continued up, the daughter turned once more and saw her mother ejected from her car.

"My mom! My mom! Let us out, we need to go get her!" were the screams witnesses heard as the ride came to an end.

Rosa Esparana died a terrible death that night. Less than a minute into the ride she fell 75 feet as the coaster was to make its first big descent and struck a support beam, which nearly cleaved her in half. Her remains thudded onto a tunnel roof. It took firefighters more than an hour to find and recover all of her.

The accident brought some attention to Texas's weak inspection system for amusement park rides and the dangers faced by heavier riders, but no significant changes were made. The ride shut down for less than a year.

The New Addiction Treatment. David A. Patterson Silver Wolf, Oxford University Press. © Oxford University Press 2021.
DOI: 10.1093/oso/9780197601372.003.0003

Rosa's family sued Six Flags and Gerstlauner Amusement Rides, which manufactured the cars. Both companies filed cross claims and blamed each other.

Rosa's death and the costs associated with her million-dollar lawsuit were, as far as Six Flags was concerned, an unfortunate failure, but part of the cost of doing business. The new-and-improved Texas Giant reopened a year later. It had different seat restraints but was otherwise unchanged.

It is a truism to say that no one, in any endeavor, is perfect. Failures occur, mistakes happen, and not every outcome is positive.

But what is an acceptable failure rate?

If your airline or amusement park had a 99 percent success rate, you would never board a plane or a roller coaster. With a 1 percent failure rate, planes would be regularly falling out of the sky, and roller coasters leaving their tracks.

If your orthopedic surgeon tells you she has a 99 percent success rate, you will probably go ahead with that hip replacement. If she does three or four hundred surgeries per year, that means only three or four go sideways— pretty good odds.

But when you hear that the artificial hip you're about to receive has a 1 percent failure rate (which it probably does), you'd be wise to ask yourself, given the 350,000 artificial hips that have been implanted over the last year or the millions over the last decade, if your hip might be among the many thousands that will fail. Suddenly that same 1 percent failure rate looms larger.

We all expect the food we buy to be safe to eat, and, with the exception of the occasional outbreak of *Escherichia coli* infections from tainted Romaine lettuce or even rarer acts of deliberate poisoning, it is. But the U.S. Food and Drug Administration doesn't expect our food to be perfect, which is why the administration's *Defect Levels Handbook* spells out exactly how many maggots (1 per 100 grams of tomato juice) and insect parts (400 per 10 grams of ground cinnamon) or how much rodent shit (10 milligrams per pound of cocoa beans) is permitted to make its way to our supermarket shelves, home to our pantries, and into our children's mouths. And while it's disturbing to think about any impurity in our food, at the end of the day, we can, thanks in large part to government regulation, generally trust the safety of what we buy and eat.

Since no one and nothing can be perfect, what is the acceptable failure rate for the treatment of addictions?

This illness, like many other chronic disorders, is complex and difficult to treat successfully.

However, if we are to believe the data regarding successful treatment outcomes, addiction treatment has the highest failure rate in all of clinical healthcare.

For example, let us compare it with some especially challenging surgical procedures: Brain surgery is dangerous, and a craniotomy is especially scary because it requires the removal of piece of the skull to access the brain, with the skull not replaced at the conclusion of the operation. Complications from this surgery include stroke, seizures, spinal fluid leakage, and excessive swelling of the brain. The worst complication in all the various medical conditions requiring some kind of invasive brain surgery—death—occurs 26 percent of the time.[18]

The stenting of the carotid artery is even more dangerous, with a mortality rate of 32 percent,[19] even in the hands of a skilled surgeon.

Anorexia and bulimia are relatively uncommon but serious problems. Sometimes described as "the cancer of psychiatry" because they are conditions that, even with treatment, can kill. However, the mortality rate, even among people who receive treatment, hovers around 4 percent.[20]

What distinguishes the treatment of addiction from the treatment of virtually all other life-threatening conditions, from asthma to anorexia and from brain surgery to bulimia, is the inconsistent use of evidence-based interventions and the almost criminally casual resignation with which failure is accepted at the nearly 15,000 addiction treatment centers around the country.

Whose fault is it?

When a patient is admitted to an addiction treatment facility and then quits after a few sessions, no one is held responsible for this negative outcome, and this quick drop out (which, from a clinical point of view, is quite likely a treatment failure) does not become part of the center's outcome data.

About 70 percent of individuals entering treatment services drop out after only two sessions.[21] It is easy to place blame for such failures on the individuals who quit attending, and of course, given the power of this disease they are trying to conquer, the urge to abandon treatment is frequently overpowering.

However, they are seeking professional help to recover from this diabolical disease, and if a treatment provider is promising that help, it should not abide early, abject failure.

If seven out of ten customers walk into a restaurant, sit down at a table, look at the menu, order a meal, take a first bite, and then make a beeline for the exit, it seems prudent to review the bill of fare, maybe taste the food, and either make some changes or find another way to make a living.

For the 30 percent of patients who do manage to continue their treatment, no one and nothing ensures that the care they are receiving is based on best or evidence-based practices.

Treatment professionals say they need the flexibility to use the clinical tools they feel will best work for their patients, and they want the room to adjust treatment approaches to their patient's unique needs.[22]

This is understandable. Each patient is a unique human being, and no single approach works for everyone; so of course, trained, experienced therapists want autonomy to employ specific interventions as they see fit. Treatment professionals value their own *practice wisdom* (i.e., professional experience) even more than they do scientific evidence.[22] This is an unfortunate triumph of anecdote over empiricism: The triumph of what *feels* best over what 40 years of research demonstrates is mostly likely to *be* best.

It is a truism that treatments and interventions supported by empirical evidence provide the highest quality of care and will improve patients' health outcomes. Yet there is no room within the treatment system infrastructure to allow for clinical flexibility and the provision of individualized care *while simultaneously ensuring that all services are supported by the best empirical evidence and real-time performance data.*

The world of addiction treatment does not ensure patients are receiving science-based care or impose *patient or therapist performance measures,* which could elicit systemic accountability.

To address this issue, we must be open to dismantling—or at least disrupting—the American addiction treatment infrastructure. Its foundation is not sound, and its current practices do not ensure high-quality, data-driven care.

Retention and completion

Regardless of the addiction treatment methods or level of care, treatment *retention* and *completion* have continually and historically been shown to significantly improve patients' overall health and wellness.[23]

Said more clearly, the better a facility is at keeping patients enrolled in care all the way through, until successful completion of their treatment program, the better are the odds of those patients achieving improved health-related outcomes.

Unfortunately, as mentioned above, most individuals who enter addiction services drop out prior to completion.[24] These patients drop out of treatment much earlier in the process than do general psychotherapy patients.[25] With so many dropouts occurring in the *first few weeks* of addiction treatment,[26] most patients receive insufficient exposure to treatment and fail to recover from their illness.

According to Eaton[27] and Hawkins et al.,[28] addiction treatment patients leaving therapy before the 3-month mark *show no significant health improvements.* Focusing treatment resources specifically toward patient retention has critical, wide-ranging ramifications. Without a planned, purposeful effort to address treatment retention rates, addiction treatment programs will continue to fall short of effectively treating this chronic illness. If patients do not stay, they have no chance of completing their program. If they do not complete their program, they are likely to continue suffering from their untreated illness.

With these retention and completion issues being so critical to the likelihood of achieving successful outcomes, it would be reasonable to expect treatment facilities to zealously monitor these two key data points.

Not only do treatment centers *not* monitor retention, but also most do not know how many days the average patient actually attends to receive services. To a cynic like me, it appears likely that they simply do not want to know because, as I have stated repeatedly, most patients stop attending treatment before hitting the 2-week mark.[29]

Completion, which implies *successful* completion, is an even more elusive figure.

A large national alcoholism study in 2001 reported that about one third of individuals treated for addiction remained clean and sober for the rest of their lives. Another third who received treatment still used drugs or alcohol, but not at as high a risk level as they did before treatment. The final third never recovered.[30]

The myth of the 2001 thirds outcome lives on today, so when asked, admissions staff at treatment centers (if they are not crowing about their 80 percent success rate) will often cite this 30 percent figure.

Even if it were correct it would be nothing to boast about. Placebos work about 30 percent of the time also. But it's not correct; analysis of electronic health records suggests that the real-world successful outcome percentage is somewhere in the low twenties.[31] We explore these data in a later chapter.

Two important facts

The first important fact is: most people who need treatment neither seek nor receive professional help.[32]

The low percentage of individuals who *do* seek help for their drug or alcohol problem do not tend to stay very long or complete their recommended course of treatment. Most drop out within their first 2 weeks of treatment, and 70 percent are gone after Week 4. While mental health treatment can improve outcomes after only a few sessions for a variety of issues, addiction treatment generally takes several months of professional clinical services to achieve a durable start on recovery.

According to almost everyone and the second important fact: addiction in America is a significant problem, perhaps our *most* significant public health problem.

In June 2019, the Pew Research Center[33] published a report on what a cross section of Americans believe to be our biggest problem. Seventy percent of respondents listed "addiction" as America's biggest problem. (This was nearly a year before the Covid-19 pandemic turned the world upside down and temporarily became this country's only focus. Before the novel coronavirus, more quietly and now under the radar as we are distracted by the pandemic, and long after we have learned to live with Covid-19, the disease of addiction kills.)[34]

What those 2019 respondents might have been connecting with would be the constant news about overdoses and the concept of drugs being part of this country's "disease of despair." Two Princeton economists, Anne Case and Angus Deaton, identified this phenomenon in a 2015 study. These economists labeled drugs, drinking, and suicide as the three diseases of despair.

A March 2017 *Washington Post* article[35] about Case and Deaton's work ends this way:

> So the theory comes back to despair. Case and Deaton believe that white Americans may be suffering from a lack of hope. The pain in their bodies might reflect a "spiritual" pain caused by "cumulative distress, and the failure of life to turn out as expected." If they're right, then the problem will be much harder to solve. Politicians can pass laws to keep opioids out of people's hands or require insurers to cover mental health costs, but they can't turn back the clock to 1955. (Appendix C)

One year later, in March 2018, the *Washington Post* ran an opinion piece, "America Is Losing Ground to Death and Despair." The article discussed a recent Centers for Disease Control and Prevention statistical analysis showing the "alarming" outcome that life expectancy in the United States fell for a second time, due to drug overdoses and suicides. This decrease in life expectancy had only happened once before and twice in all of American history, both times during pandemics (1918 and 2020).

America is in unchartered waters. Our country has never experienced a drug use crisis of this magnitude. We have become inured to daily news of opioid overdose deaths, and today, as I have said before, almost every adult knows someone who has been lost to this illness.

And the problem is so dynamically complex, our political leaders, confronted by a host of other, competing issues, do not know how to effect change. Politicians are loathe to address the kinds of problems that cannot be repaired in the span of a 2-, 4-, or 6-year election cycle, and this crisis is generations in the making and will not respond to quick fixes.

However, it is my opinion that there are reasons to be hopeful.

We know that the science is good. We know which interventions work on this specific population. We have that data, and they have been around for a long time.

We know what works. We also know that these effective interventions are not being implemented in standard care, and we know that there are few-to-zero technology-based performance measures in place.

We know therapists are not science deniers who do not care about their own performance or the performance (i.e., health outcomes) of their patients.

Moreover, we know the methods and technologies to improve care *can* be folded into standard treatment models. The science tells us that performance-based practices will improve patient care.

Change, in other words, is possible.

Too many people have been thrown off too many roller coasters for too long. We know how to keep people safe and secure for the duration of their ride, if only we have the will to learn from our mistakes.

3

How Did We Get Here?

A Brief History of Modern Treatment

In the late 1920s an investment banker named Rowland Hazard was rapidly descending into uncontrollable drinking. Having exhausted all other means of recovery, he reached out to the famous Swiss psychiatrist Carl Jung.

Jung was no stranger to treating alcoholics, as more than 10 percent of admissions to the psychiatric hospital of the University of Zurich, where Jung had trained, were wrestling with alcohol-related problems. He accepted Hazard as a patient and conducted daily sessions with him for several months. Jung's dream analysis, psychological archetypes, and whatever else Jung was practicing at that time seemed to do the trick because, a few months into his treatment, Rowland Hazard stopped drinking.

However, alcohol is a formidable opponent, and, during a planned vacation—his first time away from Jung—Hazard relapsed.

Hazard's cousin, a Pulitzer Prize–winning poet and a fellow patient of Jung's, brought him back to Zurich to see the old man (Jung was only in fifty-three in 1928, but he was a "mature" fifty-three).

Jung redoubled his efforts, but during this second analysis, he gave up, declaring that Hazard was a chronic alcoholic, beyond the reach of medicine in general or psychiatry in particular. However, Jung provided one thin ray of hope. He told Hazard that on rare occasions, alcoholics recover after experiencing some sort of life-changing, spiritual awakening or religious conversion.

Shaken by Jung's assessment and out of options, Rowland Hazard sought out the Oxford Group.

The Oxford Group was an evangelical Bible study movement founded at Oxford University by Dr. Frank Buchman after his own spiritual conversion. God revealed himself to Buchman, a Lutheran minister, and allowed him to understand the need for an emotional relationship with God's grace in order to move forward in life.

The New Addiction Treatment. David A. Patterson Silver Wolf, Oxford University Press. © Oxford University Press 2021.
DOI: 10.1093/oso/9780197601372.003.0004

Hazard's participation in the Oxford Group provided the kind of conversion experience that Jung had described, and once again, Hazard stopped drinking—and this time, it stuck.

So grateful to be free of drink, Hazard dedicated himself to helping other people like himself. A few summers later, vacationing in Vermont, Hazard heard that a former friend, a lifelong alcohol drinker named Ebby Thacher, was in jail due to drunkenness and about to be institutionalized. Hazard sought him out, shared Jung's pronouncement and his own Oxford Group recovery story, and soon a newly sober Ebby Thacher had himself become a regular member of the Oxford Group.

To pay it forward and act on the Oxford Group's core belief in evangelism, Thacher sought out the worst, most hardcore drinker he knew: a mostly unsuccessful New York stockbroker named William Wilson, whom everyone called Bill.

Thacher visited Bill Wilson's Brooklyn apartment and, though surprised by Thacher's new sobriety (they had been childhood pals and done their fair share of drinking together), Wilson was impressed with the Oxford Group's method of owning up to one's defects, admitting powerlessness, accepting help from a higher power, and making restitution to and providing service for others. Though Bill Wilson was genuinely interested when Thacher told him about Carl Jung's views about the importance of religious conversion, Wilson was still in alcohol's thrall and unable to find his way free.

Wilson continued to drink heavily, but he soon admitted himself to a local hospital and, while there, asked for his friend, Thacher, to once again outline the Oxford Group's methods. After Thacher left, Wilson sank into a depression and in abject desperation, pleaded to God for help.

Wilson later reported that at this moment, the room was filled with "a great white light," and he experienced "a new world of consciousness" with a palpable sense of "God and His world."

He stopped drinking and was discharged from the hospital. The year was 1935.

In the summer of 1935, with just a few months of shaky sobriety under his belt, Bill Wilson took a business trip to Akron, Ohio. The business went badly. Depressed and on the verge of yet another relapse, Bill Wilson felt an almost irresistible pull toward the hotel bar. Desperately fighting the urge to drink, he said to himself, "I've got to find another alcoholic."

The local Oxford Group referred Wilson to Dr. Robert Smith, an Akron surgeon known to everyone as "Dr. Bob," who'd been attending Oxford Group meetings for years while enduring periodic relapses.

Bill Wilson and Dr. Bob met and spoke for hours. So intense was their conversation that Dr. Bob invited Wilson to stay at his home. The bond between the two men grew into a movement that separated from and surpassed the Oxford Group. On that summer night in Akron, Ohio, in June 1935, Bill Wilson and Dr. Bob Smith had founded Alcoholics Anonymous, AA.

There were five elements to the original AA program. These included total abstinence from alcohol, acknowledgment of Jesus as their savior, obedience to God's will, growth in fellowship with God, and help for other alcoholics. Meetings were very spiritual, and those who joined AA often talked about the healing power of God.

To complete the circle among all these men, we fast forward to March, 1961. Carl Jung was terminally ill and would be dead in 3 months. Bill Wilson sent him a letter in which he told Jung that, in the early history of AA he and other members had read Jung's 1933 work, *Modern Man in Search of a Soul*, and were deeply moved by it. Wilson wrote to Jung, "Your words really carried authority, because you seemed to be neither wholly a theologian nor a pure scientist. Therefore you seemed to stand with us in that no man's land that lies between the two . . . [and] spoke a language of the heart that we could understand."

So as the twentieth century unfolded, perhaps starting with Jung and certainly carried by Bill Wilson, Dr. Bob, and the AA movement, spirituality became an integral part of treatment.

This was for better and for worse.

Because around the same year Bill W. and Dr. Bob were meeting in Akron, the surgeon general of the United States, Thomas Parran, identified the nation's foremost public health concerns. They were pneumonia, tuberculosis, and venereal disease. (In fact, Dr. Parran was so concerned about the effects of venereal disease, that he later went on to oversee the now-infamous Tuskegee syphilis study.)

One of the many health conditions *not* cited as preeminent by Surgeon General Parran, despite its prevalence and devastating consequences, was alcoholism.

In the years since, while medicine and science have brought tremendous advances to the treatment of pneumonia, tuberculosis, and venereal disease, addiction, to a large extent, remains locked in a time warp.

This takes nothing away from the staying power of AA. Consider that Alexander Fleming discovered penicillin just 7 years before Bill W. met Dr. Bob, and we still use it today. While we have developed better and stronger antibiotics since then, the menu of effective treatments for the disease of addiction remains appallingly small.

Addiction was first understood as demonic possession or moral failing, and it is arguable which explanation is worse. For some believers, demonic possession at least had a treatment protocol in the form of exorcism, but the moral failing perspective saw drinking as a willful act that violated socially acceptable norms, but could be overridden by individual choice.[36] The moral view of addiction remains prevalent today (e.g., "Just say no"), resulting in the shaming, stigmatizing, and ostracizing of sufferers; an ever-increasing prison population; and a slow-growing, inadequate, dedicated system of care.

Following, and not unrelated to the moral view of addiction, was the temperance movement. Temperance advocates first emphasized controlled use of alcohol, but as its use and its attendant harms widened in the late eighteenth and early nineteenth centuries, the movement morphed from advocating moderation to total abstinence. As the number of deaths, cirrhotic livers, and people (mostly men) drinking away their paychecks or beating their wives and children began to reach epidemic proportions, the temperance movement espoused the view that the cause of alcohol problems was the simple *presence* of alcohol—any alcohol.

The result, as we all now know, was that the temperance movement gained political clout and lobbied Congress to pass the Eighteenth Amendment to the Constitution, banning the manufacture, sale, transportation, and importation of all alcohol: Prohibition.

While alcohol consumption and the associated harms of drinking did indeed decrease under Prohibition,[37] the gains in improved public health were dwarfed by the unintended negative consequences. The law was hugely unpopular, impossible to enforce, and led to the creation of a vast underground, illegal marketplace for alcohol and the rise of organized crime. To this day, Prohibition is considered this country's worst failed public health experiment.

A few years after the repeal of prohibition, AA was gaining followers. Though it retained a strong religious/spiritual component, AA, largely through the pioneering advocacy of a woman named Marty Mann,[38] helped educate the public about alcoholism as an illness—a *treatable* illness. As this worldview was advanced, the moral crusade began to recede.

While the twentieth century unfolded, the medical community finally began to pay attention to alcohol problems. The nineteenth-century label of *dipsomania*, from the ancient Greek word *dipso*, for "thirst," was being replaced by a word invented in 1849 by a Swedish physician named Magnus Huss. In the twentieth century, it became the accepted way of describing alcohol problems, especially here in the United States. That word, of course, was "alcoholism."

In an attempt to study alcohol problems scientifically, the Research Council on Problems of Alcohol was established in New York City in 1938. Although the Research Council did not receive any federal funding, its work helped "de-moralize" the problem and set the stage for governmental involvement in and the creation of a federal bureaucracy around alcoholism. The first federal agency established to deal with alcohol problems was the National Institute of Alcohol Abuse and Alcoholism. Soon, and for the first time, millions of dollars were directed toward combating the disease that was killing more Americans than pneumonia, tuberculosis, diabetes, and cancer combined.

Yale's medical centers began focusing on how to effectively treat alcoholism. By 1944 Yale psychiatrists and those recovering from alcoholism started working together in order to treat alcoholism both medically and via AA's principles. People suffering from alcoholism were stabilized inside the residential hospital and once discharged, turned over to the care of AA members. This new treatment service model began to spread across the United States, metamorphosing into what we now call outpatient treatment. Treating people on an outpatient basis allowed for individuals who were unable to afford the time or money to spend 30 days living inside of a hospital to receive care after work hours.

Which is not to say that outpatient care was as powerful an intervention as was an inpatient stay. When the crack cocaine epidemic began raging through the 1980s and 1990s, resulting in the need to treat large masses of people, intensive outpatient or day treatment offered structured services for those who would have, in the past, been most appropriately directed to a 30-day stay inside a residential facility. The outcomes were poor.

Current treatment

Addiction treatment is currently designed to begin, when appropriate, with medically supervised detoxification (sometimes facilitated with palliative drugs, usually prescribed on an outpatient basis), followed by some type of psychotherapy and rehabilitation services, generally lasting from a few weeks to about 6 months. Thus, it involves both medical *and* psychological elements.

The clinical criteria for diagnosing a substance use disorder, according to the *Diagnostic and Statistical Manual of Mental Disorders (DSM-5)*[39] are the presence of two or more of the following:

1. Taking the substance in larger amounts or for longer than you are meant to.
2. Wanting to cut down or stop using the substance but not managing to.
3. Spending a lot of time getting, using, or recovering from use of the substance.
4. Cravings and urges to use the substance.
5. Not managing to do what you should at work, home, or school because of substance use.
6. Continuing to use, even when it causes problems in relationships.
7. Giving up important social, occupational, or recreational activities because of substance use.
8. Using substances again and again, even when it puts you in danger.
9. Continuing to use, even when you know you have a physical or psychological problem that could have been caused or made worse by the substance.
10. Needing more of the substance to get the effect you want (tolerance).
11. Development of withdrawal symptoms, which can be relieved by taking more of the substance.

The presence of two or three of these symptoms indicates a mild disorder; four or five symptoms indicate a moderate disorder; and six or more symptoms indicate a severe disorder.

The three levels of care for the treatment of substance use disorders are detox/inpatient, outpatient, and intensive outpatient/day treatment. All three levels include some form of group and/or individual counseling, disease education sessions, basic life skills education, and engagement with twelve-step meetings.

Detox/inpatient treatment is the highest or most aggressive/structured level of care. This usually includes residential services for detox lasting up to about 5 days with an inpatient stay lasting approximately 1 month.

Intensive outpatient/day treatment services may include daily and possibly weekend services lasting several hours per day over a period of several months.

Outpatient treatment is the least aggressive of care and is designed for those who have both stable employment and social supports.

No matter what level of care a person receives, there is no guarantee that the services provided will be effective or even helpful. The quality of care varies widely, and there is no national standard for a treatment protocol to which treatment providers must adhere.

Some programs do provide evidence-based care and hew to best practices, which I begin to define in the next chapter. Many more, do not.[40]

4

The Holy Trinity

The *USS Sultana* was a 260-foot, wooden, side-wheel steamboat that, during the Civil War, was used to transport both passengers and freight down the Mississippi River between St. Louis, Missouri, and New Orleans, Louisiana.

In April 1865, just weeks after Robert E. Lee surrendered to Ulysses S. Grant at Appomattox Courthouse, the *Sultana* was docked in Vicksburg, Mississippi, awaiting a replacement for one of its four boilers, which was malfunctioning.

While idling at Vicksburg, the *Sultana* was presented with an opportunity that was too good to pass up. With the war over, ships were needed to transport Union soldiers from where they were being held in Confederate hospitals, or in prison camps such as Andersonville, back home. The government had agreed to pay $5 for every enlisted man and $10 for every officer, so even though the *Sultana* was designed for 376 passengers, its captain, J. Cass Mason, agreed to accept more than 2,500. Rather than wait in port for a new boiler, the captain ordered the failing boiler to be hastily patched up. He figured he could get it replaced after they safely arrived in St. Louis.

Filled to six times its capacity, the *Sultana* left Vicksburg very early on April 27, 1865. It was less than 2 weeks after President Lincoln was assassinated, and, while half the divided country was deep in mourning, *all* of the divided country was focused on the war's end. No one was paying attention to the *Sultana*.

The river was high, the current was strong, and the ship was heavy in the water. The Sultana's four steam engines strained to keep it moving north, but the newly patched center boiler was not up to the task.

The ship made it a few miles north of Memphis, Tennessee, a distance of some 200 miles, when the patched boiler exploded, instantly detonating the remaining three. The damage to the center of the steamboat was catastrophic, and the force of the blast, the boiling water, the shrapnel, and the fire instantly killed hundreds.

The New Addiction Treatment. David A. Patterson Silver Wolf, Oxford University Press. © Oxford University Press 2021. DOI: 10.1093/oso/9780197601372.003.0005

The Mississippi River was cold and high from the spring thaw, and its current was overpowering. Most of those who managed to jump overboard were lost to drowning or exposure.

There were poignant stories of Confederate soldiers attempting to rescue Union soldiers who, just a month earlier, they had been trying to kill. However, there was little about the sinking of the *Sultana* that was worth celebrating.

It was then, and remains to this day, the worst U.S. maritime disaster in history. An estimated 1,800 men were lost from the Sultana, more than the number who perished aboard the *Titanic*.

The reasons for the tragedy were greed; a hasty, shoddy, incomplete repair; an utter lack of oversight; and a distracted, unconcerned general public.

There is a large body of research into what constitutes effective treatment for substance use disorders. There is evidence that a few interventions have the best odds of effecting change and, for many different kinds of patients, breaking the grip of this illness. There is, however, nothing "sexy" about these interventions. They involve neither expensive medications nor equipment. They can be delivered almost anywhere, by almost anyone. It must be noted that, for certain addictions, like opioid use disorder, there are three approved medications that may provide an essential, if temporary, assistant to treatment.

Evidence-based interventions are a prescribed series of psychological treatments that have been proven to change behavior among those struggling with addictions. Evidence-based interventions have undergone significant testing. They have been employed and investigated using controlled protocols with different population groups in different settings. Then they are retested with more than one scientist observing the results before reaching the conclusion that the treatment was successful.[41] They become evidence-based interventions when they are taken out to the field, employed again as intended, and are proven to have the same or similar results in standard practices.

Despite their demonstrable reliability and validity, and despite their relatively low cost, these techniques are not consistently being employed inside the walls of American treatment centers. And even when they *are* implemented, they often are not delivered in the way they were intended to be used (i.e., to fidelity).

Among the established intervention options that have been tested and proven, three specific approaches stand apart. There is broad consensus in the treatment community that, when faithfully administered by a skilled clinician, these three therapeutic approaches are particularly useful in initiating and supporting behavior change: *motivational interviewing, cognitive behavioral therapy, and twelve-step facilitation.*

Though a thorough exploration of how these three interventions are specifically applied is beyond the scope of this book, I provide a thumbnail sketch of each as well as a brief history of how each came to be part of the core interventions used throughout the treatment industry.

Motivational interviewing

Motivational interviewing emerged from Carl Rogers's *person-centered* approach to counseling. Rogers, who embraced Abraham Maslow's ideas about the hierarchy of needs, believed every one of us shares an ultimate motivating force, which he called *self-actualization.* Self-actualization was, according to Rogers, the inherent tendency of an organism to develop all its capacities in ways that serve to maintain or enhance the organism.[42-44]

While we all share this tendency or drive toward self-actualization, Rogers's definition suggested that self-actualization meant different things to different people.

According to Rogers, we are all born with a positive valuing process that enhances and maintains the positive things in our lives while devaluing the negative experiences that inhibit growth. With this internal process, part of our hardwired, natural design, the things and people we allow into our worlds tend to serve us well. Otherwise, Rogers believed, they would have been eliminated through a natural process of self-selection.

Frankly, it was a naïvely optimistic view of human nature, and one that squared with human experience only in the happiest and most evolved among us.

Indeed, further investigation revealed that we are not always the best judge of what is positive. Furthermore, knowing what is positive and what is negative is not always organic or intuitive. Sometimes, for example, early negative or traumatic experiences can warp what we believe is positive.

Rogers concluded that we all create our own realities. We invent our own worlds to such an extent that it is not sufficient to understand another person simply by understanding where they came from. Understanding another requires a deep understanding of their lived, internal reality—placing yourself in their individual frame of reference to get some sense of how they decode and interpret the world they inhabit.

According to Rogers, we all seek positive regard for whomever we define ourselves to be, even if we are wretched, depressed, dishonest, racist, sexist, or criminal. No matter who we think we are, we all need to be understood and accepted.

This need for acceptance is an innate, elemental part of our animal nature. Therefore, when parents respond to their children's behaviors with positive reflection, the children learn that their behavior evoked acceptance, and they try to do it again. However, if parents respond negatively, children feel some sense of rejection, and they perceive a weakening of the bond to their parents.

Before long, children learn to define themselves as others regard them. This results in individuals understanding themselves as more or less worthy, depending on the responses they received from their parents and significant others. This understanding of their social worthiness—often gained at a very early age—defines and directs the choices they make moving forward.

Given Rogers's view of human nature, it is unsurprising that he believed that the way to effect change is to provide the patient *unconditional positive regard*. For Rogers, the therapeutic relationship, achieved through *empathy* and *genuineness*, lays the foundation for helping a person to change.

Without the therapist succeeding in establishing these relationship building blocks, Rogers's therapy falls apart. Based on his theory of personality and the drive toward self-actualization, if the therapy session's atmosphere does not provide unconditional positive regard for the patient, the therapist will be unable to see the world through the patient's perspective, risking misunderstanding and the potential to inflict harm. But when skillfully executed, there are numerous studies demonstrating that it can be highly beneficial.[45]

Motivational Interviewing (MI) employs these same skills (empathy, genuineness, and unconditional positive regard) to create a therapeutic relationship—an alliance—that can support the patient's own stated desire to change. However, motivational interviewing recognizes that just because a patient expresses a desire to change, owing to the nature of substance use disorders, there is usually ambivalence. Ingesting psychoactive substances does offer its own rewards, and motivational interviewing provides a means for patients and therapists to explore and resolve ambivalence about forswearing their use. Moreover, in so doing, it helps patients find reasons to remain in treatment and, as discussed previously, the longer people stay in treatment, the more likely it is that they will find their way to sustained recovery.

Motivational interviewing is a proven practice method, able to produce results within a short period of time.[46] In a large and highly regarded randomly controlled trial, researchers[47,48] concluded that an adaptation of motivational interviewing called motivational enhancement therapy, delivered in four weekly 1-hour sessions,[49] was just as effective as cognitive behavioral therapy or twelve-step facilitation (both discussed below), methods delivered across *twelve* weekly 1-hour sessions. Although the adaptation of motivational interviewing had one third the number of sessions as cognitive behavioral therapy or twelve-step facilitation, the number of days using alcohol in the year following treatment was substantially the same across all three methods of treatment.[50] This was a significant finding that could provide additional advances in treatment techniques *if* the method can be consistently used and evaluated.

William Miller and Stephen Rollnick, the two clinical psychologists credited with developing motivational interviewing, have deconstructed it into discrete, definable, describable clinical methods that can be taught and learned.

Motivational interviewing involves the application of four basic ingredients: (a) expressing empathy, (b) developing discrepancy, (c) rolling with resistance, and (d) supporting self-efficacy. These pieces work together in order to enhance a patient's intrinsic motivation to initiate or amplify a change to healthier behavior. Patients are taught how to take responsibility for their own decisions and develop the motivation to bring about positive change. Motivational interviewing matches specific treatment strategies to the patient's existing and needed stage of change.[51] It empowers the patient to make positive changes and grow, beginning, without judgment, from wherever they are at the onset of treatment.

Back in the early 1990s, when I was a young therapist, I was trained to use motivational interviewing by studying a series of six or seven VHS tapes, manually starting and stopping at certain points to discuss the techniques employed by the therapist depicted in the simulated sessions, Dr. Bill Miller himself.

I have met Bill Miller a couple of times and can confirm that he is in the flesh as he appeared on those training tapes: preternaturally calm, nonjudgmental, and empathic.

These characteristics are key to the successful application of motivational interviewing techniques. It is essential, as Bill Miller has stated, to "be in the spirit of MI [motivational interviewing]." That is, it is essential to channel one's inner Bill Miller or Carl Rogers and display genuineness, authenticity, and caring in a nonconfrontational way, using a few specific and carefully described tools to nudge patients toward their stated goals.

Cognitive behavioral therapy

Cognitive Behavioral Therapy (CBT) comes from the 1960s work of psychologist Aaron Beck. Eponymously, it is based on the cognitive model or cognitive perspective, which postulates that our unique *understanding* of stimuli and situations in our environment directly influences the way we respond emotionally, psychologically, and physically.[52] For example, contrast your likely response to a child singing a silly song in the back seat after you have just left a fun gathering with your response immediately after an argument with your boss. In the first case, you are likely to start singing along as your shoulders jiggle in rhythm. In the second, a growled order to be quiet might be hovering on your lips as you white-knuckle grasp the steering wheel and draw your shoulders up around your ears.—Same kid, same car, same traffic outside, just a different you.

Prior to the 1920s, human behavior was assessed through an observable, behaviorist lens. Psychologists would introduce or take away stimuli and record the behavior of their subjects. What happened between the environment and the response, though, could not be fully assessed because, like with the singing toddler in the back seat, so much of our response is influenced by unobservable variables, many of which are beyond conscious awareness.

Wilhelm Wundt began to break down the workings of the human mind into its smallest parts, trying to understand these "invisible" elements. His work began to undergird Gestalt psychology in 1920s Germany,[53] with its perspective that the whole of psychological functioning is greater than the sum of multiple individual psychological processes. The rise of Gestalt psychology represented a split from the old behaviorist models of human thought, yet both offered some useful insights.

Cognitive psychology was born from a desire to connect Gestalt to the behavioral perspective. Basically, this model was created to study how our perception of the environment informed our reactions to it.

THE HOLY TRINITY   39

From the cognitive psychology model came cognitive behavioral therapy, which sought to alter the processing steps between stimuli and the response. The cognitive model *explains* our emotional (i.e., nonrational or irrational) response to a situation, while cognitive behavioral therapy endeavors to *change/improve* our unhealthy, emotional responses. For a much more detailed discussion regarding the protocols and application of cognitive behavioral therapy, you can review the work of McHugh.[54]

Twelve-step facilitation

Twelve-step facilitation was a product of AA and their twelve recovery steps.

As described previously, Bill Wilson gave AA its religious footing back in 1935. The need for a transformational religious experience to free oneself from drink was a belief Carl Jung held, and, though Bill Wilson had heard about this thirdhand, he took it seriously enough that, while confined to a hospital bed after his latest drinking binge, Wilson pursued this idea. He studied psychologist William James's book *Varieties of Religious Experience*, in which James described people being transformed after admitting complete defeat and powerlessness over their problems and turning control of the situation over to a higher power.

Bill Wilson, at the end of his tether, was able to admit his powerlessness over alcohol and give his faith over to a higher power.[55] Simply being willing to make the statement, admitting within his own mind and heart his powerlessness over alcohol, gave Wilson a similar religious experience to that described in James's book. However, as he learned a few months later on his fateful business trip to Akron, a simple statement of admission was not enough to fully, deeply achieve a long-term transformation. Bill Wilson's subsequent meeting with Dr. Bob taught him that sustained recovery would also require soul-searching, core convictions, and mutual support from other alcoholics. These became the pillars of AA, though it took Bill W. a little while to figure it out.

After his religious experience in the hospital, Wilson joined the Oxford Group as a means of continuing the kind of support he thought he needed. This was a Christian group founded on purity, honesty, and confession-style group meetings. The group had six basic, formal assumptions. These six assumptions were tweaked and modified, and some of them would become part of the twelve-step process. They included the ideas that (1) human beings are sinners; (2) human beings can be changed; (3) confession is a pre-requisite to change; (4) the changed soul has direct access to God; (5) the age of miracles has returned; and (6) those who have been changed are to change others.[56]

Wilson developed the twelve steps for his own recovery program, and it became his personal mission to sober-up alcoholics. He was disappointed during his early years to realize that exactly none of the people he tried to help found sustainable sobriety. However, when he added the Oxford Group's reliance on peer guidance and peer support, success followed.

Today, while twelve-step facilitation has its origins in the same principles as the twelve steps of AA, it is based more on science and less on religion.

Which is not to say that Bill W.'s twelve steps have been utterly rewritten or rejiggered. Much of the original language remains, and there still is some-thing about them that feels as if they come from another time.

As a formal process, twelve-step facilitation utilizes a written manual out-lining standardized procedures to take for each step.[57] Twelve-step facilita-tion therapy is widely used, and variations of twelve-step facilitation have begun to be used for treating other addictive disorders as well.

Like the other two evidence-based interventions, twelve-step facilitation is not easily adopted. There are elements of this intervention that, to people with modern sensibilities and/or robust defense mechanisms, are difficult or impossible to embrace. Some, for example, chafe at any notion of a "higher power." Others reject the idea that they are "powerless" over their addiction.

Patients in the throes of active addiction do not instinctively grasp for a way out. The illness is telling them to continue as they are, despite the terrible consequences. So merely following a motivational interviewing or cogni-tive behavioral therapy training script or telling someone about these twelve steps that were written in the near-century-old Alcoholics Anonymous Big Book is laughably insufficient.

The juice . . . the horsepower . . . the fulcrum . . . the means by which these three—and all other—evidence-based psychotherapeutic interventions manage to creep into a patient's mind and gradually alter their attitudes, beliefs, and behavior is *empathy*.

Bill Miller, the founder of motivational interviewing, has reported that without empathy, motivational interviewing is no more effective than giving a patient a self-help book to read.[58]

Motivational interviewing, cognitive behavioral therapy, and twelve-step facilitation can be easily learned. Empathy—advanced accurate empathy—cannot. Learning to accept and understand and feel for a patient who is likely to mislead or lie, likely to miss scheduled appointments, likely to stiff you, likely to smell and look bad, and likely to ignore, insult, or belittle you and your efforts, is something that can't be acquired through role playing, a classroom lecture, or YouTube videos. Further details on applying this intervention can be viewed in the work of Brown and colleagues.[59]

Do front-line therapists use these evidence-based interventions?

These three therapeutic approaches to addiction treatment have clear, distinct, formalized methods of application and scientific evidence to back up claims of effectiveness, yet most therapists in the field are relying on weak, anecdotal data: their past successes with other patients and the things they tried with those individuals that seemed to work. Many put their practice experience above 30 years of social science literature, and many still employ a *wing and a prayer* approach to treating patients.

This is not because therapists do not want to be as effective and as helpful as possible. Indeed, that is why these dedicated and generous souls picked this profession. They certainly did not do it for the money, and they did not do it for the prestige, status, or fame. They become therapists and choose to work in the addiction field because they want to make a difference. They want to help.

In the middle of the worst drug epidemic in modern American history, therapists' caseloads have increased as resources have decreased. A new therapist in the field of addiction treatment, who has a 4-year college degree and virtually no experience working with patients in desperate need, maintains a large, complex caseload.

Worse, because the entire addiction treatment system—from chief executive officer to therapists—is not held responsible for patient outcomes, interventions might be selected based on unimportant or undependable influences, such as the therapist's gut feeling or mood. Alternatively, they might have recently read about an interesting approach in the popular press that fits more with their own beliefs about this illness. Unfortunately, these varied, sometimes idiosyncratic, methods are demonstrably unhelpful.

This *science–practice gap* (so named in 2006 by the Institute of Medicine Committee on the Quality of Health in America[60]), exists in an overwhelmed system where front-line therapists with heavy caseloads on extremely tight schedules, operate with too little oversight.

Within this environment, sometimes un- or undertrained (and almost always underpaid) therapists are given absolute dominion over how to treat the many different people they encounter every day. Therapists are expected to work with *whomever* is admitted to their program, irrespective of the therapists professional training or personal background.

So, consider some of the variables a therapist must consider when a new patient is added to their calendar: gender and sexual preference; race and ethnicity; age and stage of life; diagnosis and co-occurring disorders; medical and social supports; employment status; criminal justice involvement. Is the individual homeless? Do they have a family? Are they attending voluntarily, or were they brought in against their will? What is their substance of choice? What is the last date of use? Are they intoxicated/using right now? Is detox required, and, if so, for how long? Are co-occurring disorders present?

Taking all of these factors and more into account, front-line therapists have both the power and the autonomy to decide which therapies should be used, whether scientifically proven or not.[61,62] Once the counseling office door closes, no one is looking over the shoulder of the therapist and either compelling them to treat their patients according to prescribed guidelines or cautioning them to avoid proscribed guidelines. It is not a recipe for success.

When I was a young therapist, I sometimes tried to convince my supervisor that a patient was not suitable for me and my caseload. While cases with obvious potential conflicts of interest or blurred boundaries (e.g., a patient who was an acquaintance or neighbor) were quickly reassigned, the rules of engagement changed when, for example, I expressed discomfort working with a person who viscerally reminded me of my abusive father. To my disappointment (and likely to the detriment of the patient), I was told to "figure it out."

Rather than acknowledge I might not be the best-equipped therapist to help a specific patient, I was told it was my professional duty to work through my own issues. Basically, I had to take all comers, ready or not. Moreover, this remains true for most therapists—especially those in understaffed and overburdened publically funded programs—working today.

The inconsistency or infrequency with which evidence-based interventions are used in the treatment of addictions is finally getting some attention at the national level. The *Adoption of NIDA's Evidence-Based Treatments in Real World Settings*,[4] a report from the National Institute on Drug Abuse, recommends that, along with developing and adding new interventions to the current list of developed evidence-based interventions, the treatment field must investigate ways to more effectively and consistently implement evidence-based interventions in real-world settings.

The report from NIDA is an important first step, and there are hopeful signs that the treatment field is beginning to move in the right direction. But time is of the essence.

The problem is not a lack of effective interventions; it is their insufficient deployment. The majority of treatment centers do not use the big three in a concerted, focused, organized way, yet at the same time, many of these treatment facilities and therapists mistakenly believe they are providing high-quality, state-of-the-art care. They are not. They are flying by the seat of their pants.

In addiction treatment programs, there could be greater accountability and effectiveness in the system if we focused more specifically on the evidence-based intervention model. It is much easier to track the progress and success of a program that trains its workers on one, two, or three empirically proven practices and tries to implement these select practices throughout the program's entire menu of clinical services. By focusing on proven practices, therapists can become adept at using those processes appropriately, patient outcomes can be measured to ensure effectiveness, and treatment facilities can greatly improve overall success rates. Unfortunately, although the big three evidence-based interventions lead to similar outcomes, there is a lot of pushback from therapists when they feel as if their choice of interventions is being constrained, especially when they are also told they will be called to account for their patient's health-related outcomes.

Whenever I have conveyed this viewpoint inside of treatment programs, it's been painfully obvious that the idea of being held accountable for patient care sends chills down the spines of many therapists and the systems that employ them.

Given their high failure rates it is easy to understand why. Facing dismal chances of success, it is a rare individual who volunteers for accountability when, for generations, they have been able to avoid it.

Still, since most therapists entered the field with a sincere desire to help, many will willingly agree to anything that has a reasonable chance of improving their patient's current situation.

One of the more vocalized themes of opposition to adopting a systems-wide shift to treatment that only uses the few widely investigated and proven practices is that it needlessly limits the therapist's autonomy to offer therapy using their own past practice experiences (i.e., practice wisdom). Unhappily, front-line clinical therapists generally, and particularly those engaged in addiction treatment services, use their practice wisdom—their time on the job—as an argument against evidence-based interventions and manualized therapy. Reducing their repertoire of clinical skills to just a single or a few evidence-based interventions just *feels* wrong to them.

If they have been practicing for a long time, they *do* have some success stories. Moreover, since they have been going by their gut for so long, they have come to trust their instincts.

Each patient is a unique individual, with a unique set of problems. Even under the strictest instructions to follow a prescribed set of approaches, a skilled therapist will use their intuition in the service of helping.

The goal, however, is not to go so far down the evidence-based black hole that they introduce inconsistency in practice and an inability to track results. While practice wisdom does have some value, without validated measures and specific, replicable treatment performance measures, progress will be thwarted.

Remember the *USS Sultana* and the reasons for that tragedy: a shoddy, incomplete repair; a lack of oversight; and a distracted, unconcerned general public.

This is the tragedy that is occurring in our addiction treatment industry.

5

The Best-Laid Plans

On August 22, 1965, Janet and Ron Reimer, Canadians living in Winnipeg, became the parents of identical twin boys. They named them Bruce and Brian and, after a routine, unremarkable hospital stay, brought them home.

Though otherwise healthy, by the time the twins were 6 or 7 months old, they were having trouble urinating. The boys were diagnosed with phimosis, a mostly benign condition that generally goes away on its own. But to provide an immediate cure, the parents were told to bring the boys back to the hospital and simply have them circumcised.

The pediatric urologist decided to forgo the use of a scalpel or other blade and instead opted for electrocauterization, a newer method in which high-frequency current running through a handheld instrument generates sufficient energy and heat to simultaneously cut tissue and stop bleeding.

Both boys were sedated, and the urologist began working on Bruce. The cauterizing needle was switched on, and as the physician applied it to Bruce's foreskin, there was a terrible malfunction. An electrical surge went through the cauterizing instrument, and, with a loud pop and flash of light, the smell of seared flesh filled the small operating theater and almost the entirety of Bruce's penis was instantly and irreparably burned.

The other twin, Brian, was spared circumcision and, without intervention, his phimosis resolved itself in a matter of months. However, Bruce's life would be forever changed by this genital mutilation. In the following years, he and his parents became unwitting subjects in a malign research study, designed and personally overseen by the preeminent sex researcher of the time.

Concerned about how a life without a penis would affect their son, the Reimers were desperate for help and guidance. But in mid-1960s Canada, several decades before Google, they were not coming up with much. Then, one afternoon Janet Reimer saw the famed Johns Hopkins sex researcher, John Money, being interviewed on television. She thought they had found their saving grace.

Money had become an academic superstar and media darling by advancing the idea—which seemed intuitively correct at the time—that

The New Addiction Treatment. David A. Patterson Silver Wolf, Oxford University Press. © Oxford University Press 2021.
DOI: 10.1093/oso/9780197601372.003.0006

gender and sexual identity were determined by one's upbringing and environment. In the nature-versus-nurture debate, the mainstream view was that nurture was preeminent.

Money believed that gender was a societal construct, malleable from an early age, and when Janet Reimer called his Baltimore, Maryland, office and told him about her twins, he knew he'd just found the researcher's mother lode.

Here were identical twins growing up in the same family. They shared genetic makeup, environment, and parental upbringing. Bruce would be the test subject who would undergo gender reassignment surgery and be raised as a girl, while his identical twin, Brian, would be raised as a boy. It was the perfect way for John Money to prove his theories.

Following his gender reassignment surgery, Bruce Reimer was renamed Brenda. His parents were instructed to raise him as a girl and never to tell either of their twins about what happened.

Throughout his childhood, Bruce/Brenda Reimer received annual checkups from Money. His twin brother was also part of Money's research on gender in children, and, as Reimer reported much later in his adulthood, both boys were subjected to embarrassing and humiliating, sexually provocative exercises that were, on more than one occasion, photographed by Dr. Money.

Though always calm and professorial when meeting with their parents, Reimer later reported that Money would heap verbal abuse on the boys if either he or Brian resisted complying with the doctor's often inappropriate suggestions.

In the early 1970s, in Money's published work and media interviews (where he referred to Bruce/Brenda Reimer as the "John/Joan case"), Money described Reimer's transition as successful and claimed that Bruce/Brenda's girlish behavior—facilitated by his parents buying him dresses and dolls and encouraging all signs of femininity—stood in stark contrast to his brother's boyishness. Dr. Money used, and later was accused of misusing and possibly falsifying, the data he was collecting from the Reimer twins to ratify his beliefs on gender identity (a term Money coined) and how "nurture" can prevail over "nature."

John Money's research in the John/Joan case provided justification for thousands of sex reassignment surgeries for children with abnormal genitals.

It all made perfect sense. Money's findings were intuitive. They reflected what most people believed at the time. Unfortunately, for the Reimer family and the untold number of children who received similar treatment, it was all wrong.

Contrary to Money's description of the John/Joan case, Bruce Reimer experienced severe gender dysphoria throughout his life. He was bullied at school for his more masculine appearance, and despite receiving female hormones, wearing dresses, and having his interests directed toward stereotypically female activities, he always felt himself to be a boy.

Distraught by their child's misery, the Reimers came clean to their then-15-year-old child. Bruce/Brenda learned the truth about his botched circumcision and the subsequent castration, surgical creation of a vagina, and hormone treatments.

The relief he felt was enormous, but so too was his sense of betrayal. Within weeks, Reimer assumed a male identity, taking the first name David. By age 21, he was receiving testosterone therapy and undergoing multiple surgeries to remove his breasts and reconstruct a penis. When he was 25, he married a woman.

However, this sad story does not have a happy ending.

Mental illness was present in the family. Reimer's unmutilated, unreassigned twin brother Brian suffered from schizophrenia and died from a drug overdose in 2002. Life is complicated, and it is impossible to know how much his childhood spent as John Money's experimental subject permanently scarred Bruce/Brenda/David. However, what *is* known is that on May 2, 2004, Reimer's wife told him she wanted a divorce. Two days later, he put a gun to his head and committed suicide. David—formerly Brenda and born as Bruce—Reimer was 38 years old.

Data do not always support the ideas we believe to be true. They do not always support the things we *wish* to be true. And they do not always support the things that common sense tells us *ought* to be true. In addition, when good data are distorted or ignored, we drift further and further away from understanding or being able to effect change in the world we live in.

I know these things because I have spent my entire professional life immersed in data, and during that time, I have been led to several unintuitive conclusions that the majority of the scientific community has ignored.

I have authored nearly one hundred articles on a variety of topics, many related to addiction and recovery, in peer-reviewed journals, and one question in particular has vexed me since I began working in this field back in the 1990s. In my search for answers, I found myself falling into some unexpected rabbit holes.

The quest for answers

Back in 2006, I was a new faculty member at the University at Buffalo, State University of New York, working on a large research study. We wanted to know why evidence-based interventions were not being fully used in standard care.

I was not the only person in the country interested in this topic. As I began my own work, I came across the works of Dr. Charles Glisson at the University of Tennessee. Glisson and his team of researchers were also investigating barriers to using evidence-based interventions. On the hypothesis that "bad" (their word) organizational cultures and climates created barriers to implementing evidence-based interventions,[63] they'd developed a tool, the Organizational Social Context, to measure culture and climate in social service agencies and test their theory.

Glisson defined culture as something distinct from climate, but he believed both could be measured and, by breaking *culture* down into the subscales of Proficiency, Rigidity, and Resistance and *climate* into the subscales of Engagement, Functionality, and Stress, he set out to evaluate social service workplaces.

In bad organizational cultures, employees do not keep up with the latest science and practices (proficiency); they must adhere to a large number of strict rules (rigidity); and they are resistant to change. In a bad work climate, employees don't feel much meaning or purpose in their work (engagement), do not know their role, and do not feel supported by their peers (functionality) and feel isolated or emotionally exhausted (stress).[64]

None of this was exactly revolutionary. Anyone who had ever worked anywhere would agree that different workplaces offer different cultures and climates, and some are better than others.

The more audacious claim from Glisson and his team was their certainty that they could accurately measure culture and climate within dynamic systems that are always changing. However, his Organizational Social Context survey tool, consisting of over one hundred questions, which scored organizational culture and climate along his six identified subscales, was believed to do just that.

Though it took several years, thanks in large part to a ton of federal research grants that gave him the wherewithal to kick the tires and make several adjustments along the way, his Organizational Social Context survey eventually proved to be reliable.[65]

So based on common sense and his own life experience, Glisson believed that bad cultures and climates would be bad for those served by these workplaces because, Glisson theorized, bad cultures and climates would block, or at least inhibit, both innovation and the widespread use of evidence-based interventions.

This was an exciting time. It appeared that Glisson's work was going to improve the effectiveness of all kinds of social service agencies by identifying and removing a significant barrier to change. There seemed to be limitless potential for improving these kinds of workplaces if their inner mechanisms could be measured, identified as being in need of a boost to culture or climate, and changed for the better. This, I believed, would open the floodgates for new, evidence-based interventions and better health outcomes.

Bad cultures and climates blocking innovations made so much sense. Moreover, a bad organization, as identified by Glisson's survey, could be made good again.

At around the same time but on the other side of the country, a professor in California named Greg Aarons had developed a tool to measure therapist attitudes toward evidence-based practices, postulating that the individual clinician attitudes—not organizational climate and culture—would determine the likelihood of implementing evidence-based interventions.[66]

Dr. Aaron's survey, the Evidence-Based Practice Attitude Scale, consisted of a mere 15 questions.[67] It had four dimensions: (1) *Requirements* assessed the likelihood that a therapist would adopt a new evidence-based intervention if that intervention was required by a superior. (2) *Appeal* measured the likelihood the worker would adopt a new evidence-based intervention if the worker's colleagues were happy with it or the evidence-based intervention was appealing to the therapist, made sense, and could be used correctly. (3) *Openness* assessed how amenable the therapist was to adopting new interventions. (4) *Divergence* measured how much their valuation of science diverged from their valuation of clinical experience.

Not only did Aaron's survey capture therapists' attitudes about evidence-based interventions (irrespective of their work environment), it was brief, easy to administer, and simple to score. In contrast, Glisson's survey was an unwieldy 105 questions and had to be sent to his research group in Tennessee for scoring and interpretation.

I was happy to join the ranks of those looking at barriers to the implementation of evidence-based interventions. In my own work, I wanted to understand why front-line therapists were not using evidence-based interventions in their usual practices. Therefore, in my studies at the University at Buffalo, I incorporated both Glisson's Organizational Social Context and Aaron's Evidence-Based Practice Attitude Scale tools. I figured, if nothing else, I would be able to test and lend support to the validity of what these two scientists were finding in their research.

We did various studies of social service organizations in upstate New York, which the interested (and exceptionally motivated) reader can read in their entirety.[66,68–74]

One study focused on measuring culture and climate at several social services organizations in Buffalo with Dr. Glisson's Organizational Social Context survey and determining how the workplace affected the implementation of evidence-based interventions. In organizations with bad cultures and climates (as measured by the Organizational Social Context), we were investigating whether therapists would have significantly lower rates of using the new intervention than would therapists working in good environments.

In the second study, our research team collected both Glisson's culture and climate data and Aaron's therapist attitude data from what was then the largest provider of family/child services throughout New York State. From their fifty-five different clinic locations, approximately 1,200 therapists delivering dozens of different programs for families and maltreated children, we collected a tremendous amount of data.

Glisson's already published and already established literature indicated that bad cultures and climates would create barriers to evidence-based intervention implementation, so that is what we expected to find. Instead, a very different picture emerged. We discovered that these real-world social service programs, which were measured by Glisson's tool as having bad cultures and climates, *were* able to implement evidence-based interventions.

Incredibly, the programs using evidence-based interventions had *significantly poorer culture and climate scores* than those not using evidence-based interventions.[75] Our large study, which had bigger sample sizes than Glisson's, showed that it was actually the *worst* cultures and climates that were most often using evidence-based interventions.

This made no sense, so we searched for explanations. First, we theorized that the programs with bad cultures and climates must have been *mandated* to use evidence-based interventions.

Nope. This was not the case.

Next, we theorized that therapists using evidence-based interventions must have had poorer attitudes toward the evidence-based interventions they were using, resulting in bad working conditions.

The answer was no again. Users and nonusers of evidence-based intervention held similar attitudes.

We then did further analyses of Aaron's scale to be sure it was valid and reliable.

It was.[76]

Because we had dozens of different worksites in our study, we looked at specific activities that might affect culture, climate, and attitudes in a way that might skew the data. For example, we hypothesized that programs requiring therapists to physically restrain children would report much poorer working environments than those problems where staff did not have to restrain kids. Common sense would suggest that physically restraining the children you hope to help would negatively affect the workplace's culture and climate.

Nope. There were no significant culture and climate differences between programs with zero restraints and programs with the highest reported number of instances of physically restraining youths.[77]

Finally, reasonably sure we were getting accurate, if puzzling, results, we investigated Glisson et al.'s other theory, that bad culture and climate would negatively affect patient outcomes.[65]

Again, our results were different. Programs in our study that, according to Glisson's measurements, had bad cultures and climates produced successful patient outcomes. And to make it even more baffling, the worse the culture and climate, the *better* the patient outcomes.[72]

It turned out that, *irrespective of culture and climate, the programs using evidence-based interventions got better results.*[78] Positive working conditions, while probably important to employees (and to Glisson), did not seem to affect patient outcomes. To be most effective with patients, the preeminent factor was the therapists' willingness to stick to their knitting and utilize known, evidence-based interventions.

Our findings were counterintuitive, and though they added something important to the canon of knowledge about the implementation of evidence-based interventions, they were virtually unpublishable.

Glisson at that time was a darling of National Institutes of Health funders. His Tennessee-based research was raking in millions of federal grant dollars every year, and he was publishing quite a lot in respected journals. The same journals were considerably less enthusiastic about publishing our contradictory findings.

A couple of studies by unknown researchers that challenge established knowledge generally do not and probably should not upset the apple cart. Dr. Glisson devoted much of his professional efforts to understanding and measuring organizational culture and climate. I considered him then and now to be an elder statesman who has done much valuable work. His contributions are significant, and many employees in many social service organizations have enjoyed improved working conditions after undergoing Glisson's analysis and structural recommendations. What remains un-. known is whether or not any of it has made a material difference in patient outcomes.

My team's early baffling findings have helped inform my—and in the years since, my students' and community partners'—views about how best to implement evidence-based intervention's in real-world settings.

They have also helped me maintain a healthy skepticism about the validity of and permanence of any accepted "common-sense" belief. And perhaps in today's [early 2020] world, where many facts are labeled fake, and much that is fake becomes fact, it's never been more important to base our knowledge on actual data and to test those data.

Because sometimes, as was the case with the case of John Money's sex research and the roots of gender identity, what we are taught and what we think can turn out to be nothing more than dogma, promulgated by one charismatic or influential personality.

So, back to the implementation of evidence-based interventions.

If culture and climate do not matter, what does?

When I was trying to make sense of our confounding data, I had access to the dozens of therapists who were part of one of my funded studies. I knew that a handful of high implementers were among the many who resisted regularly using evidence-based interventions, so I went back and spoke with the few who most readily embraced and constantly deployed evidence-based interventions with almost every patient on their caseload.

Surprisingly all of their responses centered on one basic personality trait: *conscientiousness*. Conscientiousness has been a reliable predictor of worker behavior[79] among employees described as "hard workers," "goal oriented," and "motivated."

These therapists believed that they had been given a job to do, and it was part of their internal belief system to accomplish it. They said things like, "This is part of my personality. . . . Given a task to do, I do it." Or, "This was something I was supposed to do."

Conscientious employees asked to perform a task in a certain way did what they were asked.

Although the sample only consisted of a small number of therapists among the many who were involved in the study, the fact that they all possessed the same personality trait jumped out at me as, if nothing else, at least a hint.

Until then, I, like many other researchers in this space, was focusing on system-level factors to explain why evidence-based interventions were not being used. While variables such as culture, climate, morale, leadership, teamwork, and workplace satisfaction were all being examined, hardly anyone was directing their attention to the actual people, the front-line "adopters." Yes, Aaron's work did assess individual attitudes, but only in the service of understanding how systemic factors affected them or their own "attitudes" toward an intervention.

It seemed to me that most researchers—and the federal agencies funding them—were barking up the wrong tree.

Untold hours of time and untold millions of dollars were spent investigating systemic and organizational factors when, at the end of the day, it was and is the responsibility of the trained therapist who, bound by both a desire to help and a code of professional ethics, is obliged to use whatever interventions science says are most effective.

So it does seem that investigating individual-specific characteristics that are related to implementation success, and making sure people with those characteristics or traits are delivering programs and services, would be more fruitful than studying how or why some organizational cultures are worse than others.

When you or your loved one is ill and needs an effective, research-proven treatment, the healthcare provider is not permitted to offer system-level excuses when they fail to deliver the goods. They are not allowed to say, "Well . . . you see . . . the work environment here is pretty toxic; there's no leadership, the team members doesn't work well together, it is my attitude that these interventions do not work, and the morale here is very low. Therefore, I just could not provide the kinds of interventions that are proven to be effective. However, once we get our organizational issues fixed and all the barriers to high-quality care have been removed, I will do better. In the meantime, unfortunately, I realize your loved one is still sick and will probably die, and I feel real bad about that."

Implementing evidence-based interventions

To ensure that conversations like that don't ever take place, I have offered several suggestions to facilitate the successful implementation of evidence-based interventions.[80]

Contrary to much established literature, I contend that certain organizational factors characteristic of "bad" cultures and climates could in fact be beneficial when implementing evidence-based interventions in *real-world settings*.

For instance, overly rigid organizations are generally considered to be bad[81] places to work. However, a certain amount of rigidity is necessary to ensure that new evidence-based interventions or other best practices are implemented.

Also, researchers have indicated that factors such as a therapist's educational level, educational discipline, and an open attitude show few or (at best) mixed impacts on whether evidence-based interventions are implemented.[70] But, it's also true that, as compared with other front-line clinicians, those with degrees in social work, and especially those just getting started in the profession, have some of the best attitudes toward evidence-based interventions. Further, therapists who are measured to be open to using new interventions and those who have grit offer the best profiles of evidence-based intervention adopters.[80,82]

The moral of the story here is that there are myriad reasons why organizations and individual therapists resist evidence-based interventions. Not all of these reasons are intuitive or seem discernible using common sense. So the better we understand all relevant factors and encourage educators, treatment providers, and other stakeholders to hire and retain those professionals who are ready, willing, and able to deploy evidence-based interventions, the more likely it is that we can improve outcomes that, today, are woefully poor.

Community-based and private addiction treatment centers are in the business of providing services, not conducting research. Most do not have the time, resources, or inclination to carry out empirical investigations or even simple program evaluations. They need partners who have the motivation and the means to help.

They need universities.

Community–academic partnerships

It is safe to assume that most major cities in the United States that have a medical school also have a university–teaching hospital nearby. Every university I ever set foot in had a medical school with a hospital sitting next to it.

The idea of a medical doctor not being trained at their university hospital is unthinkable. These teaching–learning–research organisms are dynamic and so successful that these systems exist all around the world.

Medical schools have clinical relationships with hospitals and clinics. Schools of dentistry have their own dental clinics. Psychiatry departments are aligned with university mental health clinics. Physical therapy programs train their students in their own orthopedic rehab clinics. Even beauty schools and barber colleges offer places for their students to learn their trade.

The educational system that produces the most therapists in America— schools of social work—do not have their own clinics. Social work programs send their students to someone else's clinics.

Because social work programs do not follow the model of almost every other professional education program, they are deprived of the benefits that come with having an internal teaching–learning–research system. Such collaborations provide a win–win–win situation: Social work graduate schools need community partners to carry out their mission of research, teaching, and services; community-based treatment programs need academic partners to analyze data and study outcomes; and patients need to be treated in a high-quality, science-informed system of care.

While I will go into more details how community–academic partnerships are key to addiction treatment's future in the final part of the book, I want to briefly explain some findings that came from our own Community Academic Partnership on Addiction (CAPA).

This is a unique partnership between Washington University in St. Louis' Brown School of Social Work and several St. Louis area agencies that provide a variety of addiction-related services.

The motto of CAPA of "Bringing science to service" and our coalition of the willing provide a strong, stable environment for teaching, learning, and research. Our past work together provided the opportunity to understand what is happening (or not happening) on the front line of treatment services.

The first thing we wanted to know was whether local therapists were using interventions that were supported by science.

We used several scales to survey several hundred front-line therapists throughout St. Louis and discovered that many of their clinical practices were not, in fact, grounded in any science. About 43 percent of what they were doing on a daily basis had, for all intents and purposes, no scientific support (Appendix D).

More troubling, perhaps, was the finding that these surveyed addiction therapists would not use an evidence-based intervention *even if it were mandated by their supervisor, agency, or state* (Appendix E). Further, they put more stock in their own practice experience (wisdom and intuition) than on science (Appendix F).[83]

So if an addiction treatment center has any hope of implementing a new evidence-based intervention, the very least they can do is to make it a job requirement, mandated at the organizational level. If left to the discretion of supervisors, fewer therapists—and probably not all the supervisors—will comply. Even better than compelling it at the organizational level, a superior strategy (in publicly funded agencies) is to inform therapists that it is mandated by *both* the agency and the state.

Even then, however, there will still be a cohort of therapists—over 20 percent, generally those with more years of experience and faith in the power of their own approach to effecting change—who will resist incorporating a new evidence-based intervention into their practice. They flat out told us that self-taught practice wisdom was more important to them than science.

Knowing we would have a group of clinicians within CAPA's member organizations who would resist adopting evidence-based interventions, we began a "using science" training campaign in an effort to persuade them. We urged agency leaders to set up certain mandates around clinical practices, and we also educated agency leaders about the personality traits of high implementers.

Despite these efforts, Community Academic Partnership on Addiction partner organizations, like most other addiction-focused programs, were slow to adopt and implement evidence-based interventions.

There are many reasons for this and, as discussed above, some are likely systemic. For example, due in part to their high failure rate, there is often poor morale among the clinical staff. When individual ideas do not match up with agency concepts or resources, and there is a poor fit between the individual therapist and the organization, there is lower investment and less inclination to learn something new. This is not conducive to successful learning and integration of evidence-based interventions.[84] And, unless the agency's leadership is *overtly* involved in setting expectations about the implementation process, new practices are not likely to be widely adopted.

With these and other insights, we have since made significant progress in understanding what organization barriers exist when systems want to implement a new evidence-based practice and what profile of therapist is both likely and unlikely to help with this effort.

Finally, we have begun implementing new technologies that measure a patient's recovery performance as well as measures the professional therapist's performance. While the bad news is that it is difficult to motivate therapists to use science-supported interventions to better help their patients, the worse news is that it is nearly impossible to convince them to embrace technology tools that will measure their own professional performance.

Much can be done to leverage the benefits of a university–community partnership that offers high-quality teaching, learning, and research. Just like most American medical schools, social work graduate programs should set up their own clinics, which would change and disrupt our systems of care— for the better.

Why it all matters

Currently, the addiction treatment system is largely failing the population it serves.

Yes, this is a cunning disease, and those suffering from it can be "difficult" patients, but a 75–90 percent failure rate cannot and should not be placed entirely at the sufferer's feet. Those providing the help should also be held responsible for generating better results.[85]

Think what could be achieved if, instead of a 75 percent failure rate, we were able to achieve a 75 or even 80 percent success rate. How many more people would be able to live happy, productive lives, raising happy, productive children who, when they grew into adulthood would not need treatment of their own? How many more people could be helped if, instead of having a revolving door into treatment, we had a revolving door out to recovery?

Behavior change is hard, and addiction is a tough nut to crack. We are a long way from achieving success even 50 percent of the time. Moreover, that 50 percent is still just a guess, like all other expressed facts about successful outcomes throughout this industry.

Even if we could guarantee that every therapist would use evidence-based interventions with every patient every time, we would still have no way to measure and monitor the effectiveness of those validated treatments. I have argued for the constant use of evidence-based interventions, but we cannot stop there because we are still missing a vital tool to make sure our services result in sustained recovery.

Along with evidence-based practices, we also need performance-based practice because evidence without proof is not evidence at all. It is just opinion.

We cannot stand idle and continue to do what we have always done. We cannot rely on the practice wisdom, folk remedies, and outright quackery that constitute much of today's addiction treatment.

We can, and must, do better.

PART II
THE SOLUTIONS

6

A Vision

Tatanka-Iyotanka was a warrior and spiritual leader of the Lakota Nation. He had killed his first buffalo at the age of 10 and, when he was just 14, earned a reputation for ferocity and skill by knocking a Crow Indian fighter off his horse with a tomahawk. He had proven to be unbeatable in hand-to-hand combat, though he sustained several significant battle scars in his lifetime of fighting.

By 1869 he was nearing 40 years of age and had been named the supreme leader of all the Lakota Sioux. Tatanka-Iyotanka had by now become both a renowned warrior and a "Wichasa Wakan," a holy man thought to have the gift of prophecy. He was also one of the fiercest opponents of U.S. government encroachment on Indian land. Using the term *Indian* by itself has, in the present day, become insensitive. It is usually expressed as American Indian or Native American. But this land and these human beings during Tatanka-Iyotanka's time did not have the word *American* attached to them or their land.

In the summer of 1876, while attending the annual Sun Dance ceremony—one of the most important ceremonies of the year—held by members of the Lakota and Cheyenne, Tatanka-Iyotanka was both participant and leader. It was said that he sliced his arms about one hundred times as a sign of sacrifice, and at some point, he entered into *another world*, what many non-Native people might call a trance.

When he returned, he reported having had a vision.

He saw American soldiers falling on the ground like "grasshoppers falling from the sky." He interpreted this to mean a great Sioux victory against the U.S. military was imminent. Others were made aware of Tatanka-Iyotanka's vision, and they gathered en masse and followed him to the land of "Greasy Grass," which is the south-central portion of present-day Montana.

They were prepared to do battle and make Tatanka-Iyotanka's vision come true. There was no love lost between the tribal nations and America's invading soldiers, and tensions were already high as the U.S. military was conducting a summer campaign, using both infantry and cavalry to force

The New Addiction Treatment. David A. Patterson Silver Wolf, Oxford University Press. © Oxford University Press 2021.
DOI: 10.1093/oso/9780197601372.003.0007

the Lakota and the Cheyenne back to their reservations. Negotiations had proved fruitless, and, just 3 weeks after the vision about the falling soldiers, the Seventh Cavalry attacked an encampment.

Tatanka-Iyotanka is better known as Sitting Bull. The land of "Greasy Grass" and the location of that encampment is better known as Little Big Horn. The Seventh Cavalry was led by George Armstrong Custer. And while the outcome is better known as Custer's Last Stand, it wasn't much of a *stand* at all. Custer and a couple of hundred soldiers showed up to fight the Lakota, Northern Cheyenne, and Arapaho. They were annihilated. They did indeed fall like grasshoppers from the sky until every last one of them had been killed.

Sitting Bull had a vision, and it inspired his followers to realize that vision.

In modern history, dreams and visions are not the principal engines of change. In boardrooms and C-suites around corporate America, chief executive officers are generally not using their sweaty, fever dreams to shape strategy or inspire performance.

Companies do, however, have "vision statements," which describe what a corporation or organization is trying to build and serve as a touchstone for future actions. A vision statement articulates the BHAG, an acronym coined by James Collins and Jerry Porras in their best seller, *Built to Last: Successful Habits of Visionary Companies*: the big, hairy, audacious goal. The vision statement, in other words, should inspire employees to dream and think big.

The vision statement of the Alzheimer's Association is, "A world without Alzheimer's."

The vision statement of the Multiple Sclerosis Society is, "A world free of MS."

The vision statement of the Leukemia & Lymphoma Society is, "Cure leukemia, lymphoma, Hodgkin's disease and myeloma."

These are BHAGs which are unlikely to come to pass anytime soon. Yet they provide a North Star and a raison d'être. No one gets very far without knowing where they are headed, and vision statements point the way.

So imagine my dismay when I learned that the vision statement for the National Institute on Drug Abuse is . . . nonexistent. They do not have one.

Or the mission statement of the Hazelden Betty Ford Foundation, the largest nonprofit addiction treatment provider in the country . . . also nonexistent. They do not have a vision statement or BHAG either.

The vision statement for the Substance Abuse and Mental Health Services Administration does exist, but it is far from inspiring. It reads: "To provide leadership and resources—programs, policies, information and data, funding, and personnel—advance mental and addiction prevention, treatment, and recovery services in order to improve individual, community, and public health."

Huh?

Successful, mission-driven organizations have appropriately ambitious vision statements, even if they are unrealistic. While others envision eliminating or curing disease, the Substance Abuse and Mental Health Services Administration has, as its overarching, supposedly inspiring vision statement, a clumsy word salad that, if they realized it might lead to—a modest *improvement*.

If, instead of addiction, the disease to be conquered were Covid-19, can you imagine the outrage, the outcry, and the outcome if the government agency charged with researching or funding that disease had such a diffident or weak vision?

"Yep, here at the Centers for Disease Control and Prevention we envision . . . a little less Covid-19 next year."

It is unthinkable.

Addiction is our most expensive public health problem, so it seems to me that if we are going to combat it and make meaningful change, we need a vision. We need a desired end state—a goal, a big, hairy, audacious goal.

Without such a vision, the treatment industry will continue to do what it has always done since the opioid epidemic first started rearing its head at the turn of this twenty-first century. It will grasp at straws, and, like George W. Bush landing on a carrier deck under a huge "Mission Accomplished" banner, it will declare victory without fully understanding the enemy or the scope of the battle.

With that in mind, the vision for the addiction treatment industry must be *transforming addiction treatment that achieves a 5-year sustained recovery rate of 80 percent.* Is this big? Yes.

For every addiction treatment program in America to achieve this goal would require a very big change and coordinated effort. It would mean that almost every treatment program across this nation stop doing what they are currently doing and start doing things they have never before done. It will require our government and every employer, higher education program, as well as communities and families to be actively engaged in this illness.

Is it hairy?

Most certainly it is. It will require a total reframing of this illness and its treatment. It will require the introduction of technologies and the demand that every treatment program show and share their treatment data and outcomes.

Is it audacious?

Yes. It is defiant, daring, and bold, tinged with a little impudence and disrespect for the status quo. Jumping from about a 30 percent success rate to an 80 percent rate for a complex, chronic illness seems both brazen and aspirational. But that's only because most people don't know that there already exists a treatment for substance use disorders that, at 78 percent, is tantalizingly close to hitting the 80 percent success rate.

Unfortunately, this very successful treatment system only serves a select few Americans. If you are among them and you have a diagnosed substance use disorder, the probability of achieving this big, hairy, audacious goal is almost guaranteed.

For the 99 percent of us who are not members of this prized group, we must continue to endure stratospherically high treatment failure rates while we wait for our treatment providers to undertake something that is big, hairy, and audacious.

First aid versus last resorts

Consider the national response to the opioid epidemic. When Americans began watching their children, grandchildren, parents and grandparents, nieces, nephews, neighbors, and friends dying from heroin and other opioid overdoses, addiction became real. They were not just "those people." More and more, they were people like us. They did not live in the scary inner city, and they were not a different color, ethnicity, or religion. They talked like us, they looked like us, and they lived in the suburbs with us.

Leaders and decision-makers were forced to change, at least a little. And for the first time since the Nixon administration, substance use problems began to be less of a law enforcement problem and more of a public health problem.

The argument can be made that this was patently unfair. Just 30 years earlier we treated the crack cocaine epidemic very differently, and as a result a generation of primarily people of color were arrested, adjudicated, and incarcerated. There was no attempt to offer addiction treatment to crack users, let alone treat them with compassion or understanding. They were sent to prison in large numbers to serve disproportionally long sentences.

However, it was not until illicit drug use finally reached a critical mass in majority white communities and began affecting the sons and daughters of the wealthy and powerful that things shifted.

Federal money was allocated and doled out to states. That was the forced change. It was far too little and already too late, but it was a start.

States had to figure out how best to use limited federal support, and many of them focused their efforts on reducing the number of fatal overdoses. Communities across the country began distributing naloxone (an opioid antagonist in a single-dose nasal spray form with the trade name Narcan) and began training front-line emergency professionals how to use it.

Naloxone has saved many American lives though it has done nothing to curtail the underlying problem. Consequently, many people have been revived multiple times after multiple overdoses, and the incidence and prevalence of opioid use disorders is largely unmoved.[86]

Of course, the federal monies were used not only for Narcan, an emergency first aid measure, but also (via federally supported funds) for the wider availability and use of the three medications that are demonstrably effective in *assisting* the treatment of opioid use disorder.

None of the three medications is new. Vivitrol is basically a once-per-month injection of a timed-release formulation of naltrexone, another opioid antagonist that has been around since the 1970s. The other two medications, methadone and buprenorphine (generally sold as Suboxone or Subutex), are both opioid agonists and are quite different from Vivitrol. All three of these medications have saved and restored lives. Vivitrol, though it does not reduce cravings, has helped many thousands of people achieve sustained recovery.

And by taking daily doses of methadone or buprenorphine, many, many thousands of people have become productive, loving, and loved members of society who no longer manipulate, lie, and steal to illegally obtain opioids. Instead, they can hold down a job, be a doting parent, continue their education, or do all the same things they used to do before their drug use became concerning, chronic, or compulsive.

The research literature has taught us is that (a) once someone is addicted to opioids it is extremely difficult to stop taking them and (b) to recover, one of these last two medications (methadone or buprenorphine) is an essential adjunct to behavioral therapies. In one often-cited study, when patients suffering from an opioid use disorder were prescribed methadone or buprenorphine, along with receiving traditional treatment, their overdose rates were lower than those who just received traditional treatment.[87]

Therefore, it has been repeated over and over again, that medication-assisted treatment is superior to abstinence-based behavioral treatment.

But, is this something we know for certain, or is it a persuasive bit of clinical dogma substituting for real knowledge?

A deeper dive into the medication study cited above and some subsequent research provides some conflicting data that are not widely known. For example, in the first study, those who received treatment without medications had higher overdose rates, but the researchers followed up with these folks within the short range of a few months after leaving treatment. During that brief time frame, it did seem as if medications were better at lowering overdoses posttreatment.

In a more recent study that followed patients over a longer period of time, researchers learned that those who tried to stop taking these medications—and many did—suffered higher overdose rates.[88]

In other words, a serious and little-discussed side effect of the two medications that are thought to *assist* treatment is that many people who start taking them don't, for a variety of reasons, continue taking them. Some do not like the way the drugs make them feel; others do not wish to be dependent on another opioid.

Unfortunately, once people are addicted to opioids, *including those opioids used to assist the treatment of opioid addiction*, it is very difficult and very dangerous to quit.

It remains a bit of a professional secret that the opioid agonist medications used to assist opioid use disorder treatment are themselves addictive, frequently misused, and dangerous to stop.

An opioid by any other name . . .

Opiates (morphine, opium, codeine, and heroin) refer to compounds derived directly from the opium poppy that relieve pain and create euphoria by binding to the brain's opioid receptors and releasing dopamine. *Opioids* refer to the broader class of drugs that are either derived directly from the plant or chemically synthesized in a laboratory to bind to the brain's opioid receptors. So all opiates are opioids, but not all opioids (e.g., fentanyl, hydrocodone, OxyContin) are opiates.

There are at least three types of opioid use and misuse. The first is *prescription* opioid use. These refers to the use of opioids that have been manufactured in a laboratory regulated by the Food and Drug Administration (FDA) to standards that guarantee purity and accurate dosing. These opioids are controlled (i.e., "scheduled") by the FDA and cannot be obtained without a prescription from a properly licensed health professional. Due to their powerful analgesic properties, prescription opioids are used to treat pain.

The use of prescription opioids will alter the structure and function of the human brain. Though legal and legally prescribed, these drugs are highly addictive. Misuse and sometimes even medically prescribed and supervised use can lead to the diagnosable illness known as opioid use disorder.

The second is *illicit* opioid use. This refers to the use of opioids that have been obtained illegally, without a prescription. Although the opioids might have been manufactured in an FDA-regulated laboratory and prescribed to *someone*, they might also have been manufactured in an unregulated, illegal, foreign lab with unknown and often impure ingredients, with uncertain potency and a higher risk of unintended overdose. Just as with prescription opioids, the use of illicit opioids also alters the structure and function of the human brain, which can result in the diagnosable illness known as opioid use disorder.

The third type is *medication* opioid use. This refers to the use of one of two prescription opioids approved for assisting the treatment of opioid use disorder: methadone or buprenorphine. Just like the other two types of opioid use, methadone and buprenorphine also alter the structure and function of the human brain, which—to anyone not already wrestling with an opioid use disorder because of their prescription or illicit use—can result in the diagnosable illness known as opioid use disorder.

While we might think of prescribed Vicodin is quite different from smoked black tar heroin, and we certainly think of injected fentanyl as something quite different from a daily dose of methadone, the fact of the matter is that all of these opioids act on the same regions of the brain, in much the same way.

All opioids alter the structure and function of our brains. All opioids work similarly, regardless of what we *call them.*

Which brings me back to the importance of vision.

At this moment in history, the use of methadone and buprenorphine, which are both themselves opioids, are being promoted as the "gold standard" for the effective treatment of opioid use disorder.

To a certain extent, this is both understandable and noble. We are desperately trying to rein in a runaway epidemic, and the short-term goal must be to save as many lives as possible.

However, I have been deeply distressed by a shift from medication-*assisted* treatment, to medication first, and to medication *in lieu* of treatment. There has been a push to start people on methadone or (especially) buprenorphine with neither the means to provide nor the expectation that a patient will engage in an ongoing behavioral rehabilitation program. Many advocates argue (in good faith) that stand-alone addiction treatment should disappear, and those wrestling with addictions should be treated in primary care settings.

I understand the need for desperate measures *today*. Today, we must do whatever we can to save as many people as possible. However, this should not be our vision for the future. The literature does not support medication only,[87] and we should not expect that a short-term solution designed to put a finger in a leaking dike is the same as a transformational system of care built to reach a desired end state.

If the goal is big enough, we cannot get there with half or desperate measures.

In one respect, our approach to addiction treatment resembles our approach to the war on cancer in 1971. Because scientists had a few therapies that worked to cure some forms of childhood leukemias, they believed they could apply their understanding of that one kind of cancer to the treatment of other cancers. It took decades of wrong turns before they realized that cancer is not one disease; it is hundreds of different diseases.

Medication-assisted treatment that relies on opioids *does* save lives. It may be the best we can do right now, but that does not mean it is the best we can ever do.

Addiction treatment is today what the taxi industry was in 2010, days before the first Uber ride. It is ripe for disruption, and the way we need to approach America's addiction problem does, I believe, require a total disruption from top to bottom and side to side. It starts with prevention and, along the way, will target some of the most sacred cows of clinical practice.

Sitting Bull's vision came true, but the battle of Little Big Horn was a short-lived victory for his people.

Because, unfortunately, the U.S. government also had a vision. As a result, more Army soldiers marched west. They carried better weapons, and they did not permit tribal nations to interfere with "manifest destiny" and the expansion of the country's borders from the Atlantic to the Pacific. The superior force and size of the U.S. Army permanently altered the past, present, and future of Tribal communities.

Without imagination, without setting audacious goals, and without a vision of the future for treating the disease of addictions in our nation, we are destined to continue unnecessarily producing poor outcomes for people who enter our treatment systems.

7

The Fence or the Ambulance

History has not been kind to Richard Nixon. The only U.S. president to ever resign in disgrace before his certain impeachment, Nixon and the Watergate scandal remain the gold standard by which all future corrupt or venal presidents have been measured. For more than 40 years, no one came close to Nixon's level of corruption.

When we think of Nixon, we usually think of Watergate. But he's also known for losing wars. Most notably, there was the ignominious end to the quagmire of Vietnam, euphemistically labeled "peace with honor." In addition, there are the other two wars Nixon declared himself.

On December 23, 1971, Richard Nixon declared war on cancer.

The war on cancer was described as a "moonshot," language the country certainly understood because Neil Armstrong and Buzz Aldrin had only returned from their voyage 2½ years earlier, and Nixon had not only greeted them on the deck of the *U.S.S. Hornet* upon their splashdown, but also called them on the telephone while they were on the surface of the moon.

Nixon suggested that if we applied a similar effort to curing cancer as we used to land a man on the moon, we would quickly find a cure. If it took just a decade to go from Project Mercury to Project Apollo to hearing "the Eagle has landed," then we should be able to solve the cancer riddle in half that time and get it done by the country's bicentennial in 1976.

That, of course, did not happen. It turned out to be a lot harder to cure cancer than to build a six million pound rocket, put three men inside, accelerate it to 17,432 miles per hour, orbit the earth for long enough to initiate a translunar injection and slingshot the crew out of this planet's gravitational pull toward a tiny spot on an unexplored orb in its own orbit 238,000 miles away, and then bring the crew home alive.

See, going to the moon only required a broadening and deepening of the basic knowledge and understanding already possessed by engineers, physicists, and rocket scientists. In other words, enough was already known that an enormous investment of people and money could yield massive and rapid advances.

The New Addiction Treatment. David A. Patterson Silver Wolf, Oxford University Press. © Oxford University Press 2021.
DOI: 10.1093/oso/9780197601372.003.0008

Cancer was a different beast altogether. In the 1960s, doctors and medical researchers did not understand it. There had been some recent advances in successfully arresting childhood leukemia, so the assumption was if we could cure *that* cancer, we could cure all other cancers.

As mentioned, what we know now that we did not know then was that cancer is not one disease. Cancer is *hundreds* of different diseases, governed by different disease processes involving different systems in the body.

Nearly a half century later, despite applying our best minds and the power of both government and university research dollars, surprisingly little progress has been made in curing cancer. Yes, we have made great progress in treating a small number of conditions (e.g., the twice before mentioned childhood leukemia, lymphomas, Hodgkin disease, testicular cancer), and we have developed effective screening and earlier identification of colon, cervical, and prostate cancers. But the disappointing truth is, for many other cancers, once we're diagnosed with them, they are still killing us at about the same rate they we killing us in 1971.

The war on cancer in 1971 was actually the second declared war by Richard Nixon.

Around 6 months earlier, Nixon declared war on drugs. And when we think of the war on drugs we think of a colossal failure. Thanks to one of Richard Nixon's top aides, since the mid-1990s we also think of Nixon's war on drugs as being rooted in Nixon's racism and desperate desire to keep his job.

During a 1994 interview with a reporter that was described and published in a 2016 *Harper's Magazine* article, President Nixon's policy chief, John Ehrlichman, explained:

> *The Nixon campaign in 1968, and the Nixon White House after that, had two enemies: the antiwar left and Black people. You understand what I'm saying? We knew we couldn't make it illegal to be either against the war or Black people, but by getting the public to associate the hippies with marijuana and Blacks with heroin, and then criminalizing both heavily, we could disrupt those communities. We could arrest their leaders, raid their homes, break up their meetings, and vilify them night after night on the evening news. Did we know we were lying about the drugs? Of course we did.*

Ehrlichman's interview got a lot of attention and many found it easy to believe. Nixon *was* a racist, after all. However, 1971 was fully a year before the

Watergate break-in, and Nixon's approval ratings were yet to crater. Though he was not wildly popular, when he announced the war on drugs, his job was not in jeopardy.

But Ehrlichman had an ax to grind (he went to prison, Nixon went home to San Clemente), and the interview was conducted after Nixon's death. So there was no one to suggest it might not be entirely accurate. Further, while I have no desire to be an apologist for Richard Nixon, I do believe that, in this one regard, history has treated him unfairly.

Because it seems clear that Nixon's original intention was to declare war on drug *abuse and addiction*, not on drugs themselves. Fully two thirds of the money he requested was going to be directed toward improving and expanding treatment, and toward prevention. Nixon was clear about wanting to address the demand side. He understood—and said so when he announced his plan—that it would be impossible to cut off the supply of drugs if there were people willing to buy them.

Nixon was concerned about the number of soldiers returning from Vietnam addicted to heroin, and he wanted to provide treatment for all of them. He believed and he stated explicitly that drug abuse was the country's biggest domestic threat.

However, the war on drugs did not, as we know now, target the demand side. Polling suggested that this focus on treatment would make him look "soft on crime," so he changed course, created and funded the Drug Enforcement Administration, and initiated a significant police action to cut off the supply of drugs coming into this country. Later presidents—most notably Ronald Reagan—would ramp up this war on drugs and criminalize this illness, but Nixon did get us started down this terribly wrong path.

Aside from their disappointing results, Nixon's war on cancer and his war on drugs do not seem to have much in common. One poured money into research for advances in treatment, the other into interdiction and law enforcement.

But there are at least three common threads that connect Nixon's two "wars":

Both sought to end a plague.
  Both failed.
  And neither focused on prevention.

Prevention

In the years since 1971, we have learned that the best way to reduce cancer deaths is to prevent the disease from ever occurring. Unsurprisingly, the greatest improvement in American cancer death rates is due to implementing known prevention strategies such as reducing cigarette smoking and sun exposure and increasing the availability and use of screening tests, such as Pap smears.

Deaths from skin, cervical, and colon cancers have declined. But cancer deaths related to this country's obesity epidemic and the doubling of sugar in the American diet (e.g., cancers of the pancreas, kidney, and liver) have only continued to increase, along with our weight.

The war on cancer did provide research dollars that contributed to some advances, but the cost and complexity of treating cancer has made it clear that the more we can do to prevent the disease from occurring, the better are our chances of finding effective treatments for the smaller number of varieties that remain.

Today, nearly a half-century after Nixon first declared war on drugs, with this country still in the thrall of a seemingly intractable opioid crisis, you can talk with any law enforcement professional in America, and they will all tell you the same thing. They will say: "We cannot arrest our way out of this epidemic." Put two drug dealers in prison and six more take their place. End a cartel and another moves in. Destroy a ton of illegal drugs and two more tons find their way to the street. There is too big a market and too much money at stake.

In addition, curiously, if you ask an addiction treatment professional, they will tell you that, "We will never treat our way out of this problem." The disease is too cunning, the failure rate too high, the available beds too few–no amount of money directed toward treatment will ever be enough.

So if you cannot arrest your way out, and you cannot treat your way out, it seems to me that we ought to be directing billions on billions of federal and state dollars to prevent this disease from taking root in the first place.

We know that we will never effectively reduce addiction by focusing on the supply side. For one thing, the legal substances (tobacco, alcohol, and, increasingly, marijuana) cause far more problems and cost society more than do all the illegal drugs.

To materially reduce the enormous social and personal costs associated with addiction, we need to change the attitudes, beliefs, and behaviors of our children and employ and deploy the known prevention strategies that will help kids postpone their first use of any drugs (including alcohol and nicotine) until their brains are more fully developed and better able to withstand their consciousness-altering effects.

Today we know that the central battleground is neither a hidden airfield in Central America nor a meth lab in Mexico. It is in the hearts and minds of our children.

Which begs the question: How might we prevail there?

In November 2016, U.S. Surgeon General Rear Admiral Vivek Murthy issued a landmark report, *Facing Addiction in America: The Surgeon General's Report on Alcohol, Drugs, and Health*.[40]

The surgeon general does not issue a major report very often and, when they do, it is always about a significant public health issue. Perhaps the most famous and influential example was Surgeon General Luther Terry's 1964 report, *Smoking and Health* (https://www.hhs.gov/surgeongeneral/reports-and-publications/tobacco/index.html). It reviewed more than 7,000 articles; conclusively linked smoking as a cause of bronchitis, lung, and laryngeal cancers and other diseases; led to warning labels on cigarettes and a host of other preventive measures; and is credited with saving more than eight million lives.

Therefore, when Doctor Murthy focused his 428-page report on alcohol, drugs, and health, there was reason to believe it might inform and influence the ways in which the United States tackled its most costly public health problem.

That did not happen.

The impact of this landmark report was utterly blunted by other news. November 2016 will not be remembered for the publication of Vivek Murthy's report because days before its release, an event so seismic and loud drowned out virtually all other breaking news.

Hillary Clinton's stunning electoral defeat by Donald Trump in the presidential race stole the national spotlight that month. The 2016 report did not do for drugs what the 1964 report did for smoking, and within months, Dr. Murthy was relieved of his position and was replaced by Sylvia Trent-Adams, a nurse, who, as acting surgeon general, became only the second nonphysician in history to hold the post.

Had the 2016 election and all that followed not drowned out the initial release of the report and the policy recommendations contained in it; had more Americans heard of the report, let alone actually read it; had the report been issued at a time when the executive and legislative branches of government were not dysfunctional or nonfunctional; and had the report been issued to an American public that was not being encouraged to mistrust facts and scientific evidence—had all those things been different, the possibility exists that this chapter (and perhaps this entire book) would be wholly unnecessary.

I often wonder where we might be today if, at the end of 2016, this country took the surgeon general's findings to heart and used them to inform policy.

Chapter 3 of the *Report on Alcohol, Drugs, and Health* is about prevention.

And when it comes to creating effective prevention programming, we learn that—just as with creating effective treatment programs—there exist evidence-based interventions that work if only we could broadly deliver them.

Thirty-five years of social science literature has taught us that, if we intervene early and often, it is possible to "inoculate" our children with known protective factors that will help insulate them from the known risk factors they are likely to face later in life.

The report reminds us that

- There exists well-supported scientific evidence for robust predictors (risk and protective factors) of substance use and misuse from birth through adulthood. These predictors show much consistency across gender, race and ethnicity, and income.
- There exists well-supported scientific evidence demonstrating that a variety of prevention programs and alcohol policies that address these predictors prevent substance initiation, harmful use, and substance use–related problems, and many have been found to be cost effective. These programs and policies are effective at different stages of the life span, from infancy to adulthood, suggesting that it is never too early and never too late to prevent substance misuse and related problems.
- There exists well-supported scientific evidence that communities are an important organizing force for bringing effective prevention evidence-based interventions to scale.
- There exists well-supported scientific evidence that federal, state, and community-level policies designed to reduce alcohol availability and increase the costs of alcohol have immediate, positive benefits in reducing drinking and binge drinking, as well as the resulting harms from alcohol misuse, such as motor vehicle crashes and fatalities.

- There exists well-supported scientific evidence that laws targeting alcohol-impaired driving have helped cut alcohol-related traffic deaths in half since the early 1980s.

Despite knowing these things, the amount of dollars allocated for and the number of competent educators spending part of their day delivering evidence-based prevention interventions in Grades K–12 are microscopically small.

Here in St. Louis, Missouri, there is only one not-for-profit agency devoted to providing such evidence-based programming. Every year they cobble together a budget from a patchwork of funders and manage to deliver programming to around 77,000 students. If that sounds like a lot, consider that there are nearly 500,000 school-aged kids in the region they serve, so despite their best efforts, more than 400,000 (more than 80 percent) get exactly zero programming, and many of the rest only receive some programming. Very, very few K–12 students receive the kind of comprehensive, annual sessions that build on what was taught the previous year.

If we taught reading the way we teach resiliency, we would have a country full of illiterate high school dropouts.

It is hard to know how to help shift the nation's awareness to the importance of effective substance use prevention education. Prevention does not yield immediate rewards, and, as I pointed out previously, politicians are loathe to support initiatives that don't bring results before the next election cycle.

Even when results are quantified, they are questioned. In other words, when alcohol and other drug use declines among youth (as it has, consistently, every year since mid-1990), there is no longitudinal, controlled study to conclusively determine why. Not only is there limited money for prevention programming, but there is virtually no money for sustained, high-quality research.

Much of the governmental money that is allocated for prevention does not go toward prevention. It goes toward "death prevention" and harm reduction.

Here in Missouri, much of the millions of federal prevention dollars went toward the distribution of Narcan. In 2017, a ridiculously paltry $60,000 went to fund a single, weak, evidence-based drug education curriculum for middle-school kids.

An article published in the February 23, 2020, *New York Times* (https://www.nytimes.com/2020/02/23/us/opioids-tennessee-narcan-training.

html?searchResultPosition=1) described a program recently begun in rural Carter County, Tennessee. There, health officials have embraced a program to teach young children as young as 6 years old how to administer a life-saving dose of Narcan.

This is not prevention. It is also misguided and likely to do far more harm than good. We do not teach first graders how to administer insulin, cardiopulmonary resuscitation, epinephrine, or rescue inhalers for asthma. Expecting children this young to respond to such emergencies is little more than a recipe for traumatizing them.

Nevertheless, this is how desperate we are for solutions. We look everywhere and bark up a large number of wrong trees. The desire to save lives is, of course, both understandable and noble, but without effective, broadly delivered, evidence-based prevention, we will never be able to save enough.

Those in the disease prevention business know that in order to have a measurable impact, the prevention intervention must be delivered to a large number of people at low risk of contracting the disease. You cannot restrict your intervention—whether it be a vaccine or a school-based curriculum—to a small number of people at high risk.

Reaching all or at least most of the kids is how we achieve "herd immunity." This is how we change norms and make a major, meaningful difference.

This is how we rein in the current epidemic of overdose deaths and prevent the next one from ever occurring.

Unfortunately, there is no reason to believe that our country will come to its senses any time soon. There is no major lobby like the National Rifle Association or Big Pharma demanding that our government spend money to prevent addiction in our children. It is a sad, ironic state of affairs that almost everyone recognizes the value of prevention, yet virtually no one wants to pay for it.

This, of course, is not a recent problem. Near the end of the nineteenth century, the poet Joseph Malins put the dilemma into verse. I cannot say it any better than he did.

The Fence or the Ambulance, by Joseph Malins (c. 1895)

'Twas a dangerous cliff, as they freely confessed,
    Though to walk near its crest was so pleasant;
But over its terrible edge there had slipped
    A duke, and full many a peasant.

So the people said something would have to be done,
    But their projects did not all tally.
Some said, "Put a fence around the edge of the cliff,"
    Some, "An ambulance down in the valley."

But the cry for the ambulance carried the day,
    For it spread through the neighboring city.
A fence may be useful or not, it is true,
    But each heart became brimful of pity
for those who slipped over that dangerous cliff.
    And the dwellers in highway and alley
Gave pounds or gave pence not to put up a fence.
    But an ambulance, down in the valley.

Then an old sage remarked: "It's a marvel to me
    That people give far more attention,
To repairing the harm than to stopping the cause,
    When they'd much better aim at *prevention*.
Let us stop at its source, all this mischief," cried he.
    "Come neighbors and friends, let us rally:
If the cliff we will fence, we might almost dispense
    With the ambulance down in the valley."

Better guide well the young than reclaim them when old,
    For the voice of true wisdom is calling:
"To rescue the fallen is good, but 'tis best
    To prevent other people from falling."
Better close up the source of temptation and crime
    Than deliver from dungeon or galley;
Better put a strong fence 'round the top of the cliff,
    Than an ambulance down in the valley.

8

Ties That Bind

Jan-Erik Olsson was a habitual criminal. According to the authorities, Olsson was a bomb-making expert, and, when the need arrived, he was not hesitant to use a gun.

One night, Olsson entered an empty house in his hometown of Helsingborg, Sweden. While rummaging through the house for anything of value, the owners, an elderly couple, unexpectedly walked through the front door and surprised him.

Olsson was armed, and he reached for his weapon. But before he could shoot, the husband, as a result of seeing this stranger in their kitchen, holding and adding to a pillowcase full of their belongings, moaned, clutched his chest, and dropped to his knees in an apparent heart attack.

Panicked at this sight, the wife yelled at the intruder to fetch her husband's heart medication from an upper cabinet. Jan-Erik Olsson, the outlaw intruder, could have run from the house with no risk of being followed, but instead, he sprang into action. Olsson ran across the room, flung open multiple cupboard doors, and found the man's prescription bottles. Scanning the labels, he identified and delivered the life-saving medication.

As the elderly woman tended to her ailing husband, Olsson slipped out of the kitchen, resumed his looting in the next room, and exited the home with a considerable amount of the couple's belongings.

Jan-Erik Olsson was soon apprehended for the crime and received a 3-year prison sentence. However, he also received a rare combination of infamy and notoriety for demonstrating kindness while victimizing an elderly couple.

During his time behind bars, Olsson had plenty of time on his hands. He used it to imagine and plan his next crime. He was through with the small rewards and high risks of home invasions. He would go where, as Willie Sutton famously said, the money was. Olsson was going to rob a bank: the Kreditbank in Stockholm.

More than a year later, while still incarcerated in a prison just outside of Stockholm, his good behavior earned him a weekend furlough. He made the most of it.

The New Addiction Treatment. David A. Patterson Silver Wolf, Oxford University Press. © Oxford University Press 2021. DOI: 10.1093/oso/9780197601372.003.0009

Armed with a submachine gun hidden under his jacket, carrying a large suitcase, and wearing cheap, ridiculous disguise, he entered the Kreditbank on the morning of August 23, 1973, and pulled out the gun.

Using an affected accent and speaking English in the hopes of convincing bank employees that he was American, he shouted, "The party has just begun!" (This is, of course, undoubtedly what an American visiting Sweden and robbing a bank would say.)

Most of the bank workers instinctively threw themselves to the floor. Jan-Erik pulled a small transistor radio from his pocket, turned the volume all the way up, and placed it on the bank counter. If a silent alarm were activated, and the police were dispatched the radio would be his early warning system. He had thought of everything—unless news of the bank robbery was not broadcast on the radio.

Bank employees had indeed tripped the silent alarm. The police arrived in a matter of minutes, surrounded the bank, and set up a perimeter; the area was quickly cordoned off from the public. The police knew that there were bank employees inside, so they did not immediately storm through the doors.

Jan-Erik removed rope from his suitcase and tied up a young woman named Kristin Ehnmark. She had been working at the bank a short time and was just a few months away from returning to college and completing a social work degree. Another worker, Elisabeth Oldgren, was also bound. She, like Kristin, had only worked at the bank a short while as a means of earning money to enter nursing school. Though these two women had not interacted much during their brief time as bank employees, they were about to have plenty of time to get to know one another. Jan-Erik ordered everyone else out of the bank, leaving only four—these two women, and two other employees—as hostages.

The attempted robbery of Stockholm's Kreditbank still holds the record for the world's longest hostage standoff. It was also the first hostage crisis broadcast on live television. It lasted 131 hours, just under 6 days.

During those 6 days, Jan-Erik Olsson fired his weapon several times, once hitting a police officer's hand, permanently disfiguring it. He used explosives to open a cash register and to booby-trap the hostages.

Olsson made a series of demands. Most were denied, but authorities did agree to bring his friend and prison buddy, Clark Olofsson, to the bank.

By the time Olsson was united with Olofsson inside the bank, the entire country was riveted to the drama, and Sweden's prime minister, Olaf

Palme, appeared on television, conveying his concern for the hostages and describing Olsson as being very dangerous.

To the astonishment of the viewing public, Kristin Ehnmark, the first hostage to be tied up, issued a perplexing statement. She said, "[Prime Minister] Palme, you make me very disappointed, I'm not afraid of these two men, they protect us."

It got weirder. She pleaded with Prime Minister Palme and the police to allow her to leave the bank with Olsson and Olofsson, the two men who had tied her up, wired her with explosives, robbed her of her freedom, and threatened to kill her. More than once, Kristin put herself between her kidnappers and the police, using herself as a human shield to protect them.

Early in the standoff, in order to provide food to those inside the bank, the police had drilled holes large enough to pass food through. In the end, they used those holes to deploy tear gas, and with that, the siege ended.

During her exodus from the bank, Kristin was heard shouting, "Do not harm them, they did not do anything." She was also caught on camera saying, "See you again," to Clark Olofsson.

In later interviews, the hostages spoke highly of their abductors. They explained how they were not afraid of the two criminals who held them, but mistrusted the police who wanted to save them and ultimately end their abduction. They talked about the kindness of Jan-Erik and Clark. Kristin even expressed gratitude toward Jan-Erik, stating, "When Olsson treats us well, we think he is a god."

Kristin and the other hostages' attachment to their abductors confused everyone, especially the police. The easiest explanation, and the one the police actively investigated, was that the hostages were in on the heist.

This was not the case. They had never met their kidnappers before.

Kristin was sufficiently conflicted about her own fondness for the men who had terrorized her and eventually sought professional help.

There was no name for what ailed her, but there soon would be. She and her fellow hostages suffered the same fate that befalls many victims of sexual or physical abuse. People under extreme stress, powerless to escape, sometimes develop an irrational attachment to their persecutor. It is a desperate self-defense mechanism, a powerful, irrational means of coping with an impossible situation. Arguably, it is a temporary insanity.

It is a condition that came to be named for the Swedish city in which the world first saw it on display: Stockholm syndrome.

Those in the throes of active addiction suffer from a variation of Stockholm syndrome.

Held hostage by the neurochemical changes in their brains, they pledge allegiance to the substance that is causing them great harm, threatening their health and well-being, and robbing them of everything they once held dear.

Moreover, to anyone on the outside looking in, their ongoing substance use, even after suffering so many adverse consequences, is as bizarre as Kristin's behavior in the Stockholm bank.

Finding freedom

People sometimes escape from their tormentors. Rarely are they pushed into daylight through billowing tear gas like Kristin; more often, there is a flash of sudden clarity, a come-to-Jesus moment, a last straw, a found bottom, or just a desperate, total surrender that results in release. While these flights into health occasionally happen to people in isolation, more often than not they are inspired or accompanied by another human being.

Often, it is an alliance with another that forms the bridge from sickness to health, madness to sanity, or illness to recovery.

Recovery from any health or wellness condition is likely enhanced through alliances: with medical or other healthcare professionals or with friends, family, church, or community. We increase our chances of recovery from serious injuries or life-threatening illness through our alliances with skillful surgeons; well-equipped, antiseptic hospitals; and knowledgeable pharmacists. We recover more easily from the common cold when a loved one brings us chicken soup, an understanding employer gives us paid time off, or a relative agrees to watch our children.

Recovery from substance use disorder is no different.

Of course, sufferers of addiction have the unfortunate tendency to burn bridges and sever the healthy alliances in their lives. The disease of addiction tests the patience of even the most loyal friends and loving relatives. Often, the sufferer's lying, stealing, manipulation, and maddening inability to quit drives everyone away. What remains can be unhealthy alliances with bartenders, fellow users, dealers, creditors, and codependent, enmeshed, enabling family members.

It is difficult to escape from the wilderness of this disease without a map or a guide. This is why the single most essential element of the clinical practice of treatment is the therapeutic alliance. This relationship—whether it is with a therapist, a peer counselor, or a 12-step sponsor—provides the caissons and the trusses on which a bridge from illness to recovery can be built.

In order for evidence-based interventions to be effective, they must be delivered in the context of a therapeutic alliance. This cannot be stressed enough.

I have seen too many students in my master's level addiction class operate on the mistaken assumption that, if only they memorize and execute the component parts of, say, motivational interviewing, in the prescribed manner, they will effect change in their patients. They are so concerned with "sticking to the script," with saying the things the motivational interviewing workbook tells them to say, that they miss the forest for the trees.

It is not just the intervention. To deliberately misquote James Carville during Bill Clinton's presidential campaign: "It's the relationship, stupid."

The roots of today's psychotherapy session stretch all the way back to the Viennese physician Josef Breuer (1842–1925). Around 1880 or so, while treating a patient known as Anna O., Breuer developed the cathartic method, or talking cure, for treating what were then called "nervous disorders." Breuer tends to get lost in the history of psychiatry, overshadowed by his early collaborator, Sigmund Freud. But it was Breuer who introduced Freud to Anna O. (whose real name was Bertha Pappenheim), and it was Breuer's ideas about the talking cure that were adopted by Freud and became the basis of psychoanalysis. The two men coauthored *Studies on Hysteria*, in 1895, which is considered the founding text of psychoanalysis.

Whether lying on a couch or sitting upright in a chair; whether emphasizing insight, interpretation, and transference; or focusing on all aspects of the patient's life, personality, and emotional expression, Freud and Breuer were the first scientists to understand the power of the therapeutic alliance. It is the power of two people in a room, one who has been conferred the title of healer, the other seeking help, change, or deliverance.

Of course, the therapeutic alliance was extant before science got involved. An ailing person has sought guidance from a spiritual leader for as long as there has been fire, shelter, and human speech.

Though not always stated explicitly, the importance of the therapeutic alliance is baked into therapy's DNA. Today, as in millennia past, professional therapists are trained to be healers; change agents; or wise ones. They are trained to free their patients from whatever ties bind them.

But they are not always trained how best to form a strong therapeutic alliance, and without that, they will be spitting in the wind.

I feel your pain

"You never get a second chance to make a first impression." It is an aphorism and a truism. First impressions are important and often determinative.

We see new faces every day, and, whether we are conscious of it or not, we quickly develop first-impression profiles.[89] Simply viewing a photograph of a person's face can lead us to confident assertions about that person's trustworthiness, competence, warmth, and dominance.[90,91]

A human's first-impression processing system is (or at least was) adaptive and useful for survival. Humans needed to quickly identify friend from foe. This system is automatic, requiring no conscious awareness or input.

Bill Miller, the father of motivational interviewing, was a keynote speaker at a conference we held here in St. Louis. During his presentation, he displayed two photos of a young female. He explained that the photos are identical with a single exception: The woman on the left had dilated pupils; on the right, her pupils are constricted.

According to Dr. Miller, when people viewed these photos and were asked to describe their feelings toward each one, the photo of the woman with dilated eyes received higher praise and engendered feelings of trustworthiness as well and appeared overall to be more empathic (Appendix G).

Why?

Many studies have shown that dilated pupils are associated with a number of positive attributes, and as the pupil constricts, our impression of the person becomes more negative.[92]

A therapist's ability to empathize with patients has been considered an essential aspect of therapeutic change for more than six decades. Carl Rogers[93] described empathy as a way of being with the other individual and being sensitive to the changing feelings that they are experiencing without judgment.

Being with another person and showing true empathy means setting aside your own views and values in order to enter the patient's world without your own prejudices. Or, as Feller and Cottone[94] defined it, empathy is working "within the patient's frame of reference."

Mercer and Reynolds[95] observed that the patient's perception of warmth and empathy was positively correlated with the degree to which they improved in therapy. Their study confirmed that patients with warmer and more empathic therapists had significantly more improvement than those patients working with therapists who had lower empathy ratings. Furthermore, they (and others) found that it was the *patient's own perception* of the therapist as being empathic, rather than the actual behaviors of the therapist, that held the most positive results.

During the past 20 years or so, researchers have taken a variety of approaches—cognitive in some studies, affective in others, and sometimes a combination of both[96]—to evaluate and measure empathy and the power of the therapeutic relationship. Regardless of the approach, they all relied on subjective measures, with therapists rating how well they *think* they understood their patients or patients rating how much they *felt* understood by their therapists.

The truth is that, in the decades since Carl Rogers, we have not come up with anything better. We still shoot for the same target he gave us: providing a therapeutic relationship that is empathic and free of personal judgment. All these years later, this remains essential to most every therapeutic style and technique.

And when it comes, specifically, to the value of empathy in the treatment of addictions, Moyers and Miller[97] discovered that, throughout various treatment venues, therapist empathy could predict both a patient's retention in treatment as well as their level of drinking. In other studies, worker empathy predicted drinking rates during treatment and at 1- to 3-year posttreatment follow-ups.[98,99]

Therefore, there is no more important ingredient in successful treatment of addictions than the ability to convey accurate empathy and create a therapeutic alliance quickly, with a variety of different kinds of people.

Patients wrestling with this disease are often at sea. They have no one to turn to who is nonjudgmental and deeply understanding of their illness. Their only alliances might be unhealthy and keeping them mired in drug or alcohol use. They are often desperate for a way forward and simultaneously held hostage by the chemical-induced distortions in their own thinking. When you meet them, they mistrust you and trust their captor.

You are there, in other words, to treat their Stockholm syndrome, and to do it, you must engender warmth, confidence, and trust.

Arguably, empathy and the therapeutic alliance are equally or more important than whatever evidence-based interventions are employed. As discussed in a previous chapter but worth repeating, Bill Miller's own research[58,97] demonstrated that, without accurate empathy, motivational interviewing is no more effective than handing your patient a self-help book to read.

Science or art

Empathy can be taught (to most everyone other than true psychopaths, who, by definition, are not capable of it and can, at best, simulate it). The rest of us, while unable to exert conscious command of pupil dilation, can become better at conveying understanding and establishing a strong therapeutic alliance.

Certainly one way for therapists to improve is by learning and employing the elements of the empirically supported relationship.[100] For example, a new therapist can be taught how to quickly identify the level of resistance a patient is exhibiting and matching their approach to what the patient is presenting. Therapists can be taught—they do not have to learn through trial and error—that patients with high resistance benefit more from self-control methods, minimal directedness, and paradoxical interventions, while low-resistance patients are likely to respond better to explicit advice.

Developing an alliance with patients requires both quantifiable skills and less-tangible artistry. While the former can and should be taught, the latter is what separates the good therapists from the great ones.

What skills should therapists have? What are the most effective interventions therapists should know how to efficiently deploy in practice? There are certain principles during a counseling session that should be continually monitored. For instance, therapists should give and receive feedback regarding the therapeutic relationship. Because therapeutic alliance is so important and clinically beneficial, the relationship has to be part of the regular conversation. The bond between therapist and patient—or the lack of one—cannot be ignored.

If patients disagree with any suggested interventions, it is important to address those in the moment, as it could indicate an alliance barrier. An important part of counseling, probably one of the most important, is to be aware of cues and clues to relationship threats. Missing or ignoring them are fatal mistakes.

Further, it is vital that therapists remain nondefensive and open to patient's insights into the working relationship and for therapists to actively and honestly monitor their own feelings about or inner reactions to their patients.

While many people view Sigmund Freud's work as outdated and maybe even a bit creepy, one idea has held up and continues to be discussed in today's classrooms. In the modern therapeutic relationship, the century-old phenomena of transference and countertransference remain alive and well.[101] Understanding and addressing these infectious issues as they arise during counseling sessions, without amplifying or worsening them, again requires both science and more than a little artistry.

Of course, it is critically important for therapists to know how to deliver proven practices with fidelity. However, not paying attention to and not understanding when working bonds are in jeopardy can utterly negate the potential positive effects of even the most proven evidence-based interventions.

So what are the basic human traits of an effective, empathic therapist? I think they include overt displays of empathy, explicit offerings of support and alliance, and expressions of warmth along with genuine positive regard.[102] The operative word here is *genuine*. This stuff cannot be feigned.

When I am in front of my social work graduate students, I try to encourage them to become a blend of Carl Rogers and Bill Miller, with a pinch of Robin Williams's quick, engaging wit thrown in for good measure. As the old saw goes: I want them to take their job seriously, but not themselves.

There are many historical data showing the differences in health outcomes between patients treated by a therapist with high and a therapist with low alliance measures. Alliance is effective. It is teachable and a skill that is transferable. It has had larger effect sizes than most other interventions. And, it has been tested and retested with proven results.

The widespread change needed throughout our addiction treatment industry is requiring all therapists focus on one significant thing: being expert in the art and science of building and holding a therapeutic alliance.

With it, all things are possible. Without it, nothing is.

9

First Do No Harm

Fifty-six men signed the Declaration of Independence. While the majority of Americans can name exactly none of them, many of us, thanks to his large signature (which has become synonymous *with* signatures), can name only one, John Hancock. Several of us might also think to add John or Samuel Adams, Thomas Jefferson, Benjamin Franklin, or maybe Samuel Chase. However, it would take a pretty serious history nerd (like me) to come up with *any* of the remaining fifty names. The only one I could add would be the man later known as "the father of psychiatry," Benjamin Rush, who, among his other accomplishments, was also one of the most prolific killers of the eighteenth century.

Benjamin Rush, MD, was fluent in Spanish, French, and Italian. He graduated from Princeton University at the age of 14. In 1766, he matriculated to the University of Edinburgh where, just 2 years later, he received his medical degree. Rush accompanied the Philadelphia militia during more than one battle and accepted an appointment as surgeon general of the Continental Army. Eventually he became a professor of medical theory and clinical practice at the University of Pennsylvania.

Not unlike many of his time, Rush was devoutly religious. For every disease, he knew god had a cure, and in many instances, Rush knew he would be able find that cure because he believed it was god's providence that had put him in the position to help others.

This was never more true than in the summer of 1793, during an outbreak of yellow fever in Philadelphia. Between August 1 and November 9 of that year, more than 4,000 people (out of a population near 50,000) succumbed to the disease, making the epidemic one of the worst in American history.

With thousands of residents fleeing the city, including most physicians, Rush remained behind to fight this outbreak. He managed to survive his own bout with the illness, and, when he recovered, he brought tireless energy, strong religious convictions, and formidable ignorance to his effort to save people from yellow fever.

The New Addiction Treatment. David A. Patterson Silver Wolf, Oxford University Press. © Oxford University Press 2021.
DOI: 10.1093/oso/9780197601372.003.0010

Knowing nothing about the underlying disease process or treatment of the fever, or even that it was transmitted by mosquitoes—something which would not be verified for another hundred years—Rush was grasping at straws.

He did recall that, during an earlier Yellow Fever epidemic in Charleston, South Carolina, African slaves appeared to be affected at rates lower than Whites were. Concluding they had a natural immunity, Rush suggested that the city's Black people be asked to attend to the afflicted. The call went out; Rush taught Black nurses how to treat patients and Black men how to remove corpses. The predictable result was that 240 Black men and women died, many of them only because they volunteered to put themselves in harm's way.

With nothing else in his medical bag, Rush applied one of the only therapies he knew, and in so doing he inadvertently killed far more than he ever saved, unwittingly and unknowingly becoming one of the greatest mass murderers of all time.

Benjamin Rush believed that fever was the result of too much blood flowing through too narrow blood vessels. Just as fire is the result of too much sustained friction, so too is fever. Given this understanding of fever, Rush came to believe in and practice the ancient art of bloodletting. He would remove up to 80 percent of a sick person's blood in order to reduce the volume flowing through constricted vessels. This, he believed, would reduce the friction, reduce the heat, and reduce the fever.

Given the time and the state of medical knowledge, this simple explanation of the problem and its cure made sense. So Rush went at it with a vengeance. He had to; the city was desperate for a cure, and god had put him there to deliver one.

For 90 consecutive days, Rush and his team performed the procedure on about one hundred people per day. He worked swiftly and with deadly efficiency.

Rush took careful notes, kept careful records, carefully evaluated his own practices, and was quick to publish his findings.

Though a journalist reviewed death records and noticed that death rates actually *increased* during the time Dr. Rush was draining the blood from the afflicted, it was merely assumed that the disease was spreading faster than Rush's best efforts at reining it in. No one connected Rush's attempted cure with the skyrocketing number of fatalities.

Eventually, summer turned to fall and fall turned to winter, pools of standing water froze, infected mosquitoes stopped breeding and died, and, by the end of 1793, the epidemic burned itself out. Benjamin Rush was hailed as a hero.

Into the great unknown(s)

Though there has been some sympathetic criticism of front-line addiction therapists throughout this book, along with some complaints about what they *don't* often do, one thing they do constantly, consistently, and well is collect a great deal of patient data. In addition to ongoing progress notes, these data consist of biopsychosocial and other assessment tools used to establish both a diagnosis and the outline of a treatment plan.

While there are many different assessment tools available to professionals, they almost all include information on a patient's family members and any substance use or psychiatric disorders running up or down the family tree. Most explore the patient's own substance use history, criminal justice involvement, health, mental health, living situation, and an array of other variables.

The assessment tool I was trained on (and is still in use today) was the *Addiction Severity Index*, a semistructured interview that asked about medical status, employment, and community support, drug use, alcohol use, legal status, and psychiatric and family/social status. A skilled interviewer could, in 60–90 minutes, gather information about recent (past 30 days) and lifetime problems in all of the problem areas, come up with a diagnosis, and sketch out a preliminary treatment plan.

Back in the 1990s, our agency, like all others, used hard copies of the Addiction Severity Index tool. Every paper form and all the data we collected, from the initial assessment to discharge and case closure, were stored in locked metal file cabinets.

Though our treatment program served several thousand patients a year, we really did not know the first thing about who, exactly, we were serving and how well, exactly, they were faring. We could not, for example, answer a fairly simple question like: What is the likely profile of a patient who drops out of treatment within the first 2 weeks? We did not have the capacity to quickly, let alone in real time, evaluate our own services.

Like Benjamin Rush amid Philadelphia's yellow fever outbreak, we were trying to address a serious and potentially fatal disease fully two centuries later, still with enormous gaps in our understanding of how well or poorly our treatments were serving our patients.

We observed that there always seemed to be a select few patients who completed our program, "graduated," and, as far as we knew, remained drug free. We were comforted and perhaps a bit deluded by these intermittent success stories, and, because we had an endless stream of sick people pleading to be admitted, we always felt good about being in such high demand. If someone dropped out early, well, at least we were able to admit someone new to the program and try the same things again.

Similar to Benjamin Rush, we were ignorant but confident. It was as if a crowded waiting room full of people desperate for what we were doing ratified our methods, effectiveness, and worth.

What business would stop and question the value of their services while there are long lines of customers waiting to get in?

Evidently, it was neither ours nor many other treatment centers across this nation.

Questioning the foundations of our current pillars of practice

If we were to question some of our practices—and I believe we should—then we might want to start with *case assignment*.

Case assignment is unscientific, random, and seemingly more concerned with being fair to therapists than achieving success with patients. It is based on a long-held underlying assumption that is optimistic but unproven: that therapists who are properly educated and trained can build a therapeutic alliance and achieve success with *any type of patient*. This mistaken belief is taught in professional training and practiced in professional settings. It has become dogma.

Currently, the system for assigning patients to therapists actually diminishes the likelihood of creating a strong therapeutic alliance, and it consistently shows very poor outcomes for patients.

If you are admitted to a local addiction outpatient treatment program you will be assigned to the therapist with the lowest number of patients in their caseload. This is done to ensure fairness and equity with respect to the therapists' caseloads. It's the same procedure used at discount hair-cutting salons like Great Clips. If you walk in for a haircut, you will get the first available stylist, not the person who may be best for your individual needs or the one with the most people waiting to see them.

While this assignment practice is standard operating procedure in treatment programs, there are exceptions. If, for instance, it was determined that a female patient had experienced trauma related to an abusive male, that patient would most likely be assigned to a female therapist. However, the therapist equity rule would still apply, and this new female admission would be assigned to the female therapist with the lightest caseload.

Moreover, today, what counts for a "light" caseload might be *triple* what was considered a normal or average therapist caseload 15 or 20 years ago. Today, incredibly, a therapist working a 40-hour week in a publicly funded program might have fifty, seventy, or even ninety active cases.

When I managed an outpatient treatment program in the mid-1990s, budgetary concerns forced us to raise caseloads from twenty-five to thirty. Our therapists were outraged at the thought of having to monitor, treat, and document that many patients.

From the 1990s though today, higher demand and lower reimbursement has led to an epidemic of workloads once thought to be impossibly high. I once remarked to a therapist who worked for a program serving pregnant women, mothers, and their children that today's addiction treatment industry is like the Walmart of healthcare. Without missing a beat, she said: "That's too generous. We are the Dollar Tree of healthcare." Her caseload averaged around seventy-five.

Back in 1793, without any real-time or outcome data to guide him, Dr. Benjamin Rush drained the blood from 100 people a day, saving no lives and hastening the death of many. Today, more than 225 years later, thanks in part to a random case assignment system, our front-line therapists are churning through their engorged caseloads with similarly dismal results.

Case assignment based simply on therapist caseload equity diminishes the probability of quickly establishing a strong therapeutic alliance.

Recalling we "never get a second chance to make a first impression," the first meeting with a patient goes a long way toward determining whether they will feel a connection to you and/or a belief that you can be helpful. If the treatment profession operated on the assumption that first impressions and tailored patient–therapist matching do affect the quality of therapeutic alliance or the rapidity with which it is established, cases would be assigned differently.

When talking with groups of students or professionals, I sometimes pose the following thought experiment:

I ask people to imagine that they have been married for 11 years, they have a couple of kids, and their marriage is falling apart.

I ask those who are married to raise their hand. I then instruct those in the crowd who have been married less than 10 years to lower their hands. Finally, I ask all married people without kids to lower their hands.

I point out that the few remaining individuals with their hands up are the ones who are most likely to quickly understand what this hypothetical couple with marital problems is experiencing.

It takes about 10 years to understand what marriage is really all about, and marriages change over time. Throw in a kid or two, and the marriage experiences changes again, quite significantly. The couple married for 30 years with children and grandchildren has a different relationship than they did in their first few years or even after 9 years together.

So, imagine that you are this profile of a married couple, married more than 10 years with at least one child, and you decide to see a marriage therapist. At your first session, a young man in his mid-twenties who, during introductions, reveals that he has never been married or even been in any long-term relationships greets you. He reports having no children, although you see a framed picture of him holding two cats. Referring to the photo, he says, "*These* are my two children, and boy are they a handful!"

How likely are you to entrust your marriage to this therapist?

When I query live audiences, the young therapists and social workers who do not personally fit the profile (married for more than 10 years with at least one child) are open to the idea of working with young, unmarried, childless therapists.

Those in the audience who have been married for longer than 10 years and do have children are not comfortable with the idea of seeing this young, inexperienced (at least in the ways of marriage and childrearing) clinician.

I then probe a bit. I ask if they would be more open with a middle-aged therapist who has been in a long-term relationship but never married or had children. A few are receptive.

I ask about a therapist, married for over 20 years but childless. Still more are receptive.

I ask the few holdouts—the few who remain uncomfortable with this last profile—to share why they might be reluctant to initiate marital therapy with a professional who does not meet all the criteria. Their responses are predictable.

The most common objection, in so many words, is that after more than a decade together and after a child becomes a primary focus of a couple's love and attention, their relationship becomes enmeshed with and defined by all kinds of powerful and complex connections to individual and shared experiences; emotions; hormonal and other physical changes; family; friends; and community. In addition, while these matters are extremely difficult to explain to someone who has never experienced them, empathy and understanding come easily to anyone who *has* experienced them.

So in this simple thought experiment, those people who have been married for at least 10 years and have at least one child imagine that if their marriage were falling apart and they decided to see a professional, they would *strongly prefer* someone with similar life experiences.

The good news about marriage therapy is that insured or affluent couples are likely to have autonomy and options when it is time to select a therapist, which is nice. After all, don't we and our marriages deserve the freedom of choice?

In contrast, the poor or the under-/uninsured are often seeking help from general community-based social services programs. This is where the majority of people receive treatment for substance use disorders, and these individuals are the primary focus of this book's discussion.

These patients have little choice. They will not necessarily be assigned the therapist who has the kind of similarity to or familiarity with their unique circumstances; they will be assigned the therapist with the lightest, too-heavy caseload.

Matchmaking

Rich or poor, insured or private pay, we all desire choice, and we all want a professional with whom we can form a strong connection.

Unfortunately, as I have just described, case assignment at many publicly funded treatment centers seems to serve best interests of therapists instead of maximizing the probability of a successful patient outcome. Patients are not given the therapist with whom they are most likely to feel immediate rapport; they are assigned the therapist by what is best for the treatment center.

Might this random matching (or, more frequently, *mis*matching) help explain that enormous 75 percent dropout rate across the addiction treatment industry? Might targeted matching improve treatment outcomes? And more specifically, might therapist–patient matching lead to improvement in what is arguably the most important metric: completed treatment with staff approval?

An existing body of literature examines the influence of various therapist characteristics on treatment retention. A 1994 study[103] found that the therapist's *interpersonal skills* were the strongest predictor of treatment success. In a 1991 study, it was shown that, contrary to popular opinion (and contrary to the marriage therapy thought experiment I use with my students) therapists with their own addiction history did *not* affect treatment retention.[104] The largest, nationwide study, project MATCH, concluded that clinician demographic characteristics accounted for only small variations in patient outcomes. However, this was a study that evaluated whether gender matching—female therapist to female patient—improved outcomes. It didn't.

What about the interaction between the therapist and patient's gender *and* race? There have been a few of these kinds of studies, and they have yielded inconsistent results about how these variables affect treatment completion.[103–110]

Clearly, much remains unknown. Matching on age remains virtually unexplored, and several studies noted the challenge of finding sufficiently diverse samples to properly match on both gender and race. This is especially true for non-white male patients, as the majority of treatment therapists are white females.

Researchers think this discrepancy between the racial characteristics of the providers and of the persons seeking treatment may have a negative influence on therapeutic alliance, treatment retention, and ultimately a patient's chance at full recovery. But we don't know for sure.

Given the holes in what we do and do not know about the value of matching patients and therapists, my team (consisting of people from both Washington University in St. Louis, and the University at Buffalo) and I wanted to see if matching specifically on race and gender was associated with differences in outpatient treatment completion success rates. The associated goal was to understand whether certain matching scenarios increased treatment completion rates and, if so, to identify the most beneficial combinations.

We worked with a large addiction treatment agency in St. Louis. It was our good fortune that their chief executive officer was the rare, intellectually curious leader who cared more about improving care than risking potential embarrassment if their outcomes were poor, so he was willing to share his company's electronic health records data with our researchers.

Between 2013 and 2015, we collected de-identified data on the race and gender of sixty-nine therapists and more than 2,200 patients from eleven of their outpatient programs. Race was simply categorized as either white or non-white. Gender was reduced to just male or female. A closing status of *treatment completed* was coded as *successful*, and any other closing status was coded as *not successful*.

I became interested in this because, as in the marriage therapy thought experiment, it made so much intuitive sense that matching would matter. It was hard for me to believe that a few professional development trainings or graduate coursework on cultural competence could adequately prepare a single therapist for all of the norms, customs, traditions, or shared life experiences of the myriad kinds of people they serve.

Given that gender, for example, now has a rapidly lengthening list of variations beyond male/female, how could a therapist become "competent" in all of them?

With dozens of races, religions, ethnicities, and genders and thousands of permutations, it seems unrealistic to expect that the same therapist who might best understand the perspective of, say, a person with an alcohol use disorder in a newly exiled former Hassidic Jew transitioning from male to female will do equally well with Latina single mother who suffers from an opioid use disorder after a work-related injury and lives with her aunt, sister, and toddler son in a fourth-floor walk-up apartment as with a Wall Street hedge fund manager with a nine-figure salary, leased Lear Jet, and a serious cocaine problem.

I believed patients and therapists would do best when they could quickly connect with one another. Therefore, before this study began, I hypothesized and was certain that race and gender matching would produce a higher rate of treatment success.

Data collection began, and, sure enough, it turned out that white male patients did best with white male therapists. This pairing led to a successful outcome in nearly 46 percent of all those matched cases.

In contrast, white male patients had the lowest success rate (under 10 percent) when matched with non-white male therapists.

In between those two extremes, the white male patients fared okay (32 percent success) with white female therapists and half that well (17 percent success) with non-white female therapists.

So, with white men seeking help with their addiction, like did best with like.

When I saw the success that occurred between white male patients and therapists, it made sense and supported my hypotheses. Given these results, I was convinced that non-white female patients would have greater treatment success when matched with non-white female therapists.

But this was not the case.

My hypothesis was destroyed. Counterintuitively, white male therapists had the best results with the non-white female patients assigned to them (Appendix H).

Hopes that my hypothesis would be confirmed and my results would be published started fading.

To those interested in sample sizes, tables and graphs, I refer you to the cited study itself.[111] What follows are just a few comments about our findings.

Given that we simplified our matching to two binary options (male/female, white/non-white), there were a manageable number of sixteen different combinations of race and gender. For both therapists and patients, there were only four possibilities (white male, white female, non-white female, non-white male).

Therefore, which therapist profile did best (i.e., had the highest percentage of patients successfully completing treatment) with each patient profile?

If the existing dogma that any therapist can connect with any patient is true, then patients in this study should have an equal chance at success regardless which profile of therapist they were assigned. In other words, the four different gender/race profiles of therapists should have equal success with each type patient. However, if *my* hypothesis were correct, matching therapist–patient profiles would have the highest success rates.

This was not what we found—not even close.

Yes, white male patients did do best with white male therapists.

And white female patients experienced a successful outcome with a white female therapist 23 percent of the time, while their success rates with non-white female therapists was much worse, a dismal 2.5 percent.

However, curiously, the success rate for white female patients when paired with a white male therapist was a whopping 50 percent, nearly double the rate of white women patients paired with white women therapists.

Huh? We were stunned to learn that the white male therapists did best with *all* patients. They outperformed their peers in every match scenario (Appendix I).

Each time I present these findings, I am asked to explain them. "Why," I am asked, "did the white male therapists achieve the highest success rates with all the different profiles of patients?"

I wish I had the answers, but the truth is, I do not know. Like everyone who hears them, I am not sure what, if anything, to make of these results.

It is tempting to just dismiss this finding as a one-time anomaly. Certainly, as with all other research studies with small sample sizes, there are a number of limitations and caveats.

While we collected some basic data about race and gender, there's a ton we don't know. For example, we do not know the level of staffing at any of the eleven participating clinics, so we do not know the exact, "in the moment" process by which a patient was assigned to a specific therapist. There may have been racial or gender bias by one or more people in one or more locations, and that by itself could have skewed our results.

We do not know anything about the patients or the therapists beyond their race and gender. Therefore, there is no way to know if the white male therapists were treating people with comparable socioeconomic status, co-occurring disorders, or disease severity as were the non-white and female therapists. It is quite possible the white male therapists got the "easier" cases.

As much as I hate to say it: These findings are suspect and should not be generalized beyond this sample.

Nevertheless, the one thing that does seem clear from this study is that there are outcome differences between similar and dissimilar patient–therapist pairings. While my small sample size and experimental design cannot conclusively determine which match is optimal, the work does show significant variations in success rates. This raises some very important questions about the accepted protocol for case assignments. The practice of assigning patients to the least-overworked therapist is so ingrained that there has never been a reason to change it. However, it does seems reasonable to question the belief that every patient has an equally good chance at success irrespective of resemblance to their therapist.

If you wanted to get the best possible care for you or a loved one, you might want a treatment center that would match you with the therapist you would be most likely to develop a quick rapport. Matching to optimize outcomes does seems to matter.

I must say again that it does seem to me that, in today's addiction treatment world, poor outcomes are not examined as much as they are just blamed on the patient or their disease.

This is patently unfair and terribly irresponsible. I am suggesting that it is not the patient's fault. I am suggesting that it is the fault of both the treatment providers and the educational (mostly master's-level) programs that train the therapists who work for treatment providers. I am suggesting that institutional dogma; beliefs; systems; policies; and practices are the primary contributors to these disappointing outcomes.

The usual method of case assignment must be challenged. We must also question our *reassignment* practices. Therapists can remove a patient from their caseloads only if they are related to or have some personal connection (e.g., existing friendship) or conflict of interest with them or if a case assignment triggers a past or aggravates a current life trauma.

But if the patient or therapist simply expresses dissatisfaction with one or the other, there is generally not a case reassignment. Therapists are asked to deal with patients they have a hard time connecting with; patients are discouraged from picking or switching their assigned therapist. Again, these practices are based on old, outdated ideas that, while easier on the treatment center, have not been studied for effectiveness and likely do not provide maximum benefit to patients.

We need to exhume buried data

The overtaxed, underfunded system of care continues to churn through its waiting list, providing services without real-time data.

Thirty-years ago I collected data with paper and pencil, placed forms in manila folders, and filed those folders in metal cabinets—data coffins—where they were never seen again.

Those were the old days and the old ways.

The metal file cabinets have long since been replaced by electronic health record systems. We now type into networked computers, creating electronic documents that are copied to electronic folders that are saved to the electronic health record's system.

Where, once again, they are never seen again. The biggest difference between then and now is that today we have more sophisticated and expensive data coffins.

While we do review patients' charts to make sure we are meeting state and federal compliance requirements, the treatment industry still operates without its data guiding or informing clinical practices.

Given the high failure rates, it seems self-evident that current addiction treatment approaches should be scrutinized and challenged. When, as in our study, non-white female patients had a failure rate of more than 98 percent when matched with a white female therapist, it seems ethically questionable for an agency not to collect data on, then base its case assignments on, at least in part, therapist–patient success matching. With the inability to measure real-time performance as it relates to treatment outcomes—like therapist–patient matching discussed above—outcomes will continue to be dangerously and embarrassingly poor.

Published completion rates

For making an informed choice about where to get the best treatment, what else might matter?

Knowing actual, successful completion rates might matter. Although most every treatment program collects data in their electronic health record systems, very few reveal them.

In our study, the overall completion rate for these eleven outpatient programs was a disappointing 23 percent. Using an airline industry analogy, 77 percent of their passengers do not arrive at their planned destination.

One reason is that patients frequently leave treatment prematurely. It has been repeatedly demonstrated in our scientific literature and in this book that the single biggest predictor of a successful outcome is the length of time a patient remains in treatment.[112,113]

White patients remain in treatment almost double the number of days as non-white patients (Appendix J). What explains this glaring disparity, and how to narrow it?

Is it a dearth of non-white therapists? Is it related to using different drugs? Is it connected to economic/insurance issues, institutional racism, cultural issues, and so on?

No one knows.

However, unless we can study and provide answers to relatively "easy" questions like this, we may be subjecting patients—especially our non-white patients—to the modern-day equivalent of bloodletting.

Rather than continuing to blame patients who "haven't hit bottom," "aren't ready for recovery," or "resist treatment," perhaps, if we really want to help more people and save more lives, it is necessary to monitor and evaluate therapists' performance.

Continuing to use the same, tried-and-true practices without any performance measures during and after the delivery of that practice keeps us in the dark ages of ignorance and inadvertent bloodletting. Without real-time data, a 2020 addiction treatment facility will be producing outcomes more similar to Benjamin Rush's yellow fever treatments than to other modern therapies.

Eventually, it was good data that doomed Dr. Rush and ended the practice of bloodletting. New practices were discovered and countless lives were saved.

With today's technology tools, there are no more excuses for a lack of data-driven practices. The addiction treatment world could have a variety of real-time data tools to select and direct treatments as well as identify/improve high and low performers throughout its clinical workforce.

And along the way, as both funding agencies and patients become increasingly well informed about organizational and therapist success rates, they will demand targeted case assignments and evidence-based interventions that show real outcomes.

And then, perhaps more of our troubled travelers will successfully arrive at their desired final destinations.

10

If It Works for Them, Why Not Us?

There is nothing exceptional about Paula W.'s appearance, though she looks tired. Her brow is furrowed, her face is heavily lined, and she looks like she has lived every day of her 61 years, and several hundred days beyond that. Paula's hair has turned gray. Her wired-rimmed glasses make her eyes look small, but that is hard to detect because her anxiety keeps her from looking directly at me. Dressed conservatively and professionally in a blue short-sleeved, button-down shirt, dark blue blazer, khaki pants, and unscuffed flat shoes, she is sitting in my office, avoiding eye contact.

We spend a good hour and a half together, and, during that brief time, I hear some of Paula's history and begin to understand how this ordinary-seeming woman was inching toward a ledge and beginning to fall from an extraordinary height.

Paula and her brother were in elementary school when their mother died from breast cancer. Paula's father threw himself into his work and became a successful businessperson, but when he came home from work and drank too much alcohol, he turned into a mean, abusive parent. When Paula was a teenager, she eventually learned that, in addition to his alcoholism, her father suffered from a serious mental illness. There were many clues, but all doubt was removed when her father, without perceptible signs or warning, committed suicide.

Paula's grief was complicated. She confessed to be feeling both very happy that her dad was dead, but simultaneously furious that she would never have the opportunity to confront her dad about all the abuse she and her brother had endured. Neither joy nor anger is the typical reaction to a parent's death, but it was not hard to understand why Paula might have felt both emotions.

Paula's older brother experienced a psychiatric breakdown in his twenties. Formerly outgoing and gregarious, he became withdrawn and isolated. He left college, returned to his old bedroom in their childhood home, and began consuming absurd amounts of alcohol.

Any money that was left from her father's estate was poured neat, on the rocks, or straight from the bottle into her brother's drunkenness. Alcohol,

The New Addiction Treatment. David A. Patterson Silver Wolf, Oxford University Press. © Oxford University Press 2021.
DOI: 10.1093/oso/9780197601372.003.0011

Paula's brother once told her, was the only substance—and he had tried them all—that enabled him to get through the day.

Against the odds, Paula seemed to escape the gravitational pull of her family's health woes. She went to an out-of-state college, majored in chemistry, and did well enough to consider a career in medicine. In her senior year, she took the MCAT—Medical College Admission Test—and did well enough to be admitted to a medical school.

When I met her, Paula was working as a senior anesthesiologist at the local university hospital. She had married her college sweetheart, and they were still together after 20 some years. She had a good job, a steady income, a seemingly happy marriage, and two teenaged boys she adored.

But is wasn't all peaches and cream for Paula. She was experiencing some work-related problems which were serious enough that, if she wished to retain her job, she would be required to seek immediate professional help. In addition, while she was happy with her husband, she was less content with the state of their union.

When she followed the mandate to seek assistance, Paula chose mine from a pretty long list of names, and while she never said why she had selected me, I could guess.

I did not specialize in general mental health or marriage and family issues. I was not the eating or mood disorder person; I did not work with gender dysphoria, and I did not know much about parenting. However, I was the *only* name that listed my specialty as "addiction." It was there in the big print right next to my name. So if you requested me, you wanted help with your (or sometimes your loved ones') substance use disorder.

Most of the patients who asked for me were everyday working people. They had a problem with a substance, but most of them continued to be productive at their manufacturing or warehouse jobs until—well—until they were not.

Unlike most of my other patients, Paula was not a laborer or middle manager. She was a physician, my first ever, so I was eager to meet and learn all about her.

I suppose that is part of the reason I remember Paula so well. However, the primary reason I remember her is that she was my last official patient.

I was transitioning from the direct practice world into a new profession, academia. My dissertation was almost finished, and soon I would be accepting an assistant professor position. I was going to do this evaluation on Paula, pack up my office, and head out of town.

My career was at a crossroads. And it turned out that so too was Paula's, but not in a good way.

The state medical board had frozen her medical license. She was on the brink of losing the ability to practice medicine, the only thing she was trained to do. Her career, her family, and her way of life were all in grave peril.

How had it come to this?

It is here where Paula's becomes a sad story you will have doubtlessly have heard before.

Paula's hospital had begun to notice a difference between how much morphine was being documented for patient use and how much was actually remaining. Hospital administrators quickly raise red flags when inconsistencies are found during routine medication inventory reviews.

At first, the reviewers believed the problem was benign: poor record-keeping. In an active university hospital with a kinetic emergency department, there are occasional discrepancies when inventory is checked against distribution. Overworked medical staff sometimes get numbers wrong or forget to write them down. Often, there are innocent explanations. But this time, while there was an explanation, it wasn't innocent.

The hospital tracked repeated shortages of morphine, and it became apparent to investigators that the drug was being diverted, not once or twice, but steadily, month after month after month.

In a large hospital with thousands of employees, only a select few, qualified staff members are allowed access to tightly controlled substances, so it was easy to narrow the number of suspects.

Paula was identified as the culprit and confronted.

She denied it, of course, but the hospital had overwhelming evidence and had already informed the state medical credentialing board. Paula was given two options.

Either surrender her license and no longer work as a practicing physician. Alternatively, admit to and be treated for the addiction that led to her egregious and dangerous violation of hospital, state, and federal regulations, to say nothing of the medical profession's code of ethics.

It was a stark and therefore easy choice, even for a woman who, because she was suffering from a brain disorder caused by her drug use, did not believe she had a problem.

Paula was a very sick person. It was her good fortune that hospitals are in the business of helping sick people, medical boards want to rehabilitate impaired physicians, and, perhaps best of all, her care—like all physician addiction care—would be guided by the best and most current research.

Addiction is a chronic illness, with relapse/recurrence rates similar to other chronic conditions such as asthma and diabetes.[114] Just as these conditions require many years (not days or weeks) of ongoing care, so does the proper treatment of substance use disorders.

Consider that those who sustain sobriety for 5 years enjoy a very small rate of relapse. It is analogous to a cancer patient's 5-year survival rate. After 5 years, their rate of cancer recurrence is often no greater than if they had never had the disease at all.

On the other hand, despite abundant medical literature that has consistently demonstrated increased mortality when a chronic illness—*any* chronic illness—is not appropriately treated and the patient experiences multiple recurrences/relapses,[115] most addiction treatment lasts less than a month.

Physicians in active addiction pose a clear threat to public safety. However, it takes so long to properly train medical doctors that permanently stripping them of their license to practice would create shortages and gaps in an already fragile healthcare system.

So today, every state has a Physician Health Program, a specialty care model begun in the 1970s after the American Medical Society published an article, *The Sick Physician: Impairment by Psychiatric Disorders, Including Alcoholism and Drug Dependence.*[116] The physician health program, or PHP, is designed to treat and rehabilitate any impaired doctor who agrees to its conditions. These treatment programs operate with close oversight, and unlike most nonphysician treatment programs, physician health programs are held accountable for their outcomes.

The prevalence of addiction among physicians is about 10–12 percent,[117] about the same as it is in the general public. However, while doctors experience the rate of disease as often as the rest of us, their treatment does not resemble the treatment options for everyone else.

It is a lot better—a whole lot better.

For Paula and others in the program, treatment begins with evaluation and intervention. This is a vital first act in creating a deliberate sequence of events leading to a desired conclusion. The physician undergoes a biopsychosocial assessment. Importantly, the evaluation will often include family, friends, and colleagues.

Once the evaluation is completed and the results are determined, PHP leadership, often the medical director, brings a treatment team together to discuss the full diagnostic picture of the patient along with any other "collateral" circumstances (e.g., co-occurring conditions). A plan is developed, next steps are formulated, and the team begins to populate the details of a treatment and monitoring contract.

If necessary, the physician is medically detoxified and stabilized. When treatment commences, it usually begins with about *3 months* of residential care at one of a half-dozen select residential treatment centers sprinkled throughout the United States. These programs are all required to adhere to stringent record-keeping, monitoring, and reporting standards; provide the highest levels of 360-degree clinical care; and be accountable for their outcomes.

Immediately after residential treatment, physicians begin an intensive outpatient program with individual and group therapies, twelve-step support group attendance (if they wish, at their own, closed to the general public, "caduceus" meetings, which are restricted to recovering healthcare professionals), along with other ancillary medical or mental health services.

Significantly, state physician health programs require their patients to sign a *5-year contract* detailing treatment services and consequences for noncompliance. All physicians in the program must maintain total abstinence from alcohol and nonmedical drug use. Moreover, this total abstinence policy is closely monitored through 5 years of frequent, random drug and alcohol testing. Additionally, throughout the 5 years, physicians must agree to unannounced worksite visits as well as having their colleagues and family members report on their ongoing progress.

Addiction requires long-term care. Treating it otherwise, like, say, as a problem that can be solved in 28 days or even 3 months, is not supported by *any science.*

In physician health programs, the use of pharmacotherapies—medication-assisted treatment—is the exception and not, as it is for the rest of us, the rule. According to a 2008 study that included 802 physicians in multiple programs throughout the United States, around 280 of those physicians were diagnosed as having an opioid use disorder, but only one was prescribed an opioid-based medication-assisted treatment. Several more (about seventeen) were prescribed naltrexone, an opioid antagonist, but the majority found recovery through abstinence-based treatment.[118]

Relapses are addressed immediately, aggressively, and nonpunitively. Physician health programs recognize that relapse is often a part of recovery, so physicians are not summarily expelled from the program.

Throughout these programs, relapse is not defined solely by a recurrence of substance use. There are three levels of relapse. The first level deals with missed appointments, dishonesty, or other behaviors that raise concerns. Level two relapse is reuse of substances outside the context of clinical practice hours. And level three, the highest and most concerning relapse, is substance use during on-the-job, medical practice, work hours.

Whenever relapse happens, it is addressed the way any other disease recurrence is addressed. The individual is reevaluated and treatment plans are adjusted accordingly. The level of care may be heightened. The program will redouble its efforts because relapses are not viewed as strictly an individual failing. Relapses are understood to reflect the inadequacy or insufficiency of the *treatment plan*. Obviously, relapsing physicians cannot practice medicine, but a relapse does not necessarily result in permanent job loss.

There are those who consider medication-assisted treatment the "gold standard" of addiction treatment. There are those who believe that abstinence-based treatment is antiquated and ineffective.

However for doctors, despite its general insistence on abstinence, physician health programs have a success rate, according to most investigations, of about 75 percent.[117] That's crazy good.

Most people who hear about these programs and their high success rates point out that physicians are vastly different from most people entering public treatment programs. They have a lot to lose if they do not enter treatment and comply with its demands.

This is true.

They devoted many years of hard work, often incurring a large amount of student loan debt, to obtain what is often a high-paying, high-status job. Losing it would be very hard on the physician and their family, and this motivation provides a great deal of "recovery capital."

To be sure, it is a factor, but it is one of many and does not fully explain the vast difference in treatment success between physician health programs and other treatment programs. Job loss is a powerful motivator, and that is true for *anyone* who depends on that income to support themselves and/or their families. The consequences of losing a $300,000 salary that supports a $300,000 lifestyle are devastating. However, that is true no matter the number. In fact, an argument could be made that losing a subsistence wage is even more consequential.

A 2009 study found that less than a third of doctors felt forced into treatment under threat of losing their license/jobs,[117] which is not to say that most were not pressured into seeking help; they were. But it was through the same coercion any human faces when suffering from an addiction: the love and support and/or threats and disapprobation from family, friends, or colleagues. Most impaired doctors, in other words, are not propelled into treatment by a fear of losing a paycheck; they are moved toward and supported through recovery by their community.

Physician health programs, unlike most public treatment centers, welcome the physician's community and, whenever possible, make it part of the treatment. This seems to have a salubrious effect on both initiating and maintaining sobriety.

Including the patient's family is not a revolutionary idea. When a physical injury or illness affects a family, it is common for their community to pitch in and help.

Many years ago, my youngest son spent 5 days in a children's hospital. His mom and I took turns during day and night shifts so someone could be at his side every minute. Another family member, *who lived in another state*, took time off work to help us.

This is as it should be and as it often is for physical illnesses. Children's hospitals and other healthcare providers encourage this. Hospital rooms have foldout sofa beds, and visiting hours are liberal. Health and healing are individual, family, and community concerns, and most medical facilities and physicians understand this.

Most providers of addiction treatment do not. They act as if the patient's family, until proven otherwise, is—some way, somehow—responsible for enabling or worsening the illness. Families are mostly uninvited into the addiction treatment process. Unless a facility has a standard family program on their schedule (which may not be billable), families wait for their loved one to be treated and returned.

Physician health programs consider the relationship between the disease and the patient's community differently. From the initial evaluation, PHPs include, educate, and leverage the people and relationships in the ill person's world to assist in the recovery process.

Physicians enter into a treatment program—The rest of us enter into a treatment schedule

I once had a conversation with a former U.S. Marine that has stayed with me all these years later. He was 6 feet 4 inches, lean, and heavily muscled, and though he had worked for me as a counselor for over 2 years, he had never volunteered any information about his two tours in the Gulf or any of his service medals. He was strong and silent and, I suspected, a formidable warrior.

One day, while eating lunch together and talking about the state of the world, he mentioned that America's enemies have no clue what they are up against. In that moment, I sympathized with America's enemies. If he was the typical warrior who showed up for our side, the enemy should be scared. Though he was a gentle presence in our clinic, having him and a few thousand of his fellow marines swarming an objective with a mission to destroy would indeed be intimidating.

Of course, he wanted to make a different point. He told me that the American military knows how to "project its resources" onto its enemies. And among this country's military strengths is the ability to understand and measure the enemy's capabilities. Once you know exactly what you are up against, you know what personnel, weapons, and materiel you will need to prevail, and you can then start running different scenarios, predictions, or "games" to see which resources and which sequence of deploying those resources works best to defeat the enemy.

This was a lesson I never forgot.

A guy named Joe McQuany gave me another lesson I would always remember.

Joe ran a 30-day addiction treatment center in Little Rock, Arkansas. He was an elder statesman in Alcoholics Anonymous; he once told me that, "Treatment is a sequence of events that leads to a conclusion." He pointed out how, with physical ailments, the doctor tries to diagnose/understand the problem and only then deploys the treatment plan. The healthcare provider will measure and monitor whether that illness is being effectively treated and make the necessary clinical adjustments along the way. Treating illness or disease requires an identification of the exact nature of the problem, identification of the solution, and then execution of a prescribed plan of action steps that moves from the identified problem to the solution.

I think about these two men and what I learned from them whenever I tour a new addiction treatment facility. Their words come back every time I ask a treatment center director to "tell me about your program."

Treatment directors typically hand me a weekly schedule of activities. For instance, every morning they will show me that there are groups, then a break, followed by individual counseling sessions, more groups, lunch, specialty groups, maybe some feel-good activities like yoga or swimming, and possibly some less conventional remedies like art or music or even equine therapy. They usually list the number and titles of their workforce, which will include some array of counselors, licensed therapists, community support specialists, employment specialists, peer support specialists, and sometimes a medical director.

When this happens, I think about that former Marine and Joe McQuany and very politely say, "I am wondering about your program, and you just showed me your weekly schedule. What is your *program*? What is your specific sequence of events that leads to recovery?"

Generally—well, almost always—I receive a quizzical look and no understanding of the difference between a program and a schedule.

However, it is the difference between a bunch of semiprecious stones lying randomly around the ground and a handcrafted, assembled necklace.

Today's treatment industry has some understanding of its enemy: the disease of addiction. It also has an understanding of its resources or at least its funding support and the job descriptions and abilities of the people who work in it.

Unfortunately, it has not a clue how to deploy its resources in a sequential manner that effectively and efficiently moves patients from problem to solution, from disease to recovery.

Instead, most treatment centers throw all their available resources—counseling, therapy, employment, education, and community and peer support—at every patient, in the same sequence and with the same emphases.

There is little understanding or appreciation of how each resource is connected to and supports all of the others. In military terms, it's equivalent to deploying all of America's resources to do battle at once. Ground troops are deployed at the same time airplanes are dropping bombs, the Navy is firing missiles, and diplomats are opening briefcases to start negotiating peace.

Arguably, it is this lack of customized, individualized treatment plans that contributes to a high failure rate, and, conversely, it is the individualized, highly organized, and closely monitored structure that contribute to the success of physician health programs.

Physician health programs understand their resources and how to sequentially and effectively deploy them. They know the resources of their enemy—the substance use disorder—and what it takes to win each battle on the way to victory/recovery. PHPs are neither a war on drugs nor a war on the individual. They are educated, science-supported missions to achieve 5 years of sustained recovery.

There are other addiction treatment programs with similar coercion, consequences, and structures. For example, "drug courts" exert tremendous pressure on people who are arrested and voluntarily enter this alternative-to-incarceration program. Drug courts have some of the same rules, practices, and expectations as physician health programs. There are many programs that use drug testing to monitor recovery.

However, drug courts do not come close to the physician health program's legitimate success rate. The treatment industry serving non-healthcare providers keeps about 30 percent of its patients alcohol and drug free after the usual 3 to 6 months of treatment. In physician health programs, according to the work of DuPont and colleagues' 2009 study,[117] "78 percent had completely negative urine test results throughout five years and 71 percent were still practicing medicine at the five-year point."

So, clearly, for anyone seeking the best chance of recovery from addiction, the first and most important step is to become a practicing physician.

Alternatively, perhaps there might be a way of transferring what these programs tell us about addiction treatment and bringing it to everyone.

Most addiction treatment in the United States is badly broken. In the next chapter, I offer a fix. However, most in the treatment industry will openly deride it and actively resist it.

In a way, I do not blame them. They have had a pretty sweet deal for about 85 years, and we have been willing to accept their poor outcomes by blaming the patients and the disease.

But this has to change.

Improvement in the way we treat this illness will benefit untold millions of people, prevent untold families unimaginable suffering, and save untold billions of dollars.

If we discovered an effective treatment for Alzheimer disease that worked 78 percent of the time but we only made it available to physicians, there would be rioting in the streets.

It is time we demand equal treatment rights for the equally destructive and more widespread disease of addiction.

Remember Paula W., my last official patient and the only doctor ever referred to me?

I saw her just a few times. I collaborated with her state's PHP and did not hear from her again after I transitioned into academia.

No guarantees, but I would lay good odds, about an 80 percent chance, she is healthy, sober, and still practicing medicine today.

If the 80 percent chance of sustained recovery is good enough for physicians, it should be good enough for the rest of us.

Bringing this level of addiction care to everyone will take a vision, a movement, and a serious disruption.

Note to readers

Many of the above studies on physician health programs were conducted before the opioid epidemic fully manifested itself. I wondered if their program's policies had changed with the times and are now permitting or even encouraging their physicians to recover with buprenorphine or methadone. Having participated in the National Academies of Science, Engineering, and Medicine report that supported the increased use of medication-assisted treatments[87] for everyone else, I wanted to see if this included physicians with opioid use disorders.

I contacted three state physician health program boards, including my current state of Missouri, as well as Kentucky and West Virginia, two states hit especially hard by the opioid epidemic. All three said that physicians are prescribed naltrexone (not an opioid), but "practicing physicians" were not permitted to use buprenorphine or methadone (both opioids). They claimed it was an issue of "public safety." Their policies prohibit practicing physicians from using most mind- or mood-altering substances. Physician health programs still generally require total abstinence (the few exceptions include selective serotonin reuptake inhibitors and other antidepressants).

I asked if they required total abstinence because that is what traditional treatment has long expected. I was told it was not.

They all repeated: It is a "public safety issue."

Leveraging my ignorant-of-the-ways-of-the-real-world professor status, I asked why the public would have to be protected against someone taking methadone or buprenorphine. After all, I said to these three program administrators, these are the medications being widely used to treat opioid use disorder throughout the United States and Europe.

No one could provide an answer. After long pauses from all three, they repeated their interest in public safety.

In other words, it seems that while methadone or buprenorphine are just fine for us—the people caring for your children in daycare or driving them to school in yellow buses, building your cars and homes, preparing your food, or delivering your Amazon packages—it is not okay for the physicians who are finding recovery through physician health programs.

PART III
THE NEW ADDICTION TREATMENT

11

The Twenty-Third-Century Solution

Eugene Wesley Roddenberry survived three plane crashes. Had he not, Marty Cooper might never have changed our world.

During the Second World War, Second Lieutenant Eugene Roddenberry was a pilot in the 394th Bomber Squadron of the U.S. Army Air Corps. Of the more than 80 missions he flew, many were terrifying, few were routine, and one, which never got him more than 30 feet off the ground, was life altering. On August 2, 1944, Eugene's B-17 Flying Fortress, named the *Yankee Doodle*, prepared to take off from Guadalcanal. As the fully loaded bomber hurtled down the runway, achieved enough speed to take off, and Roddenberry began to "rotate," or pull back on the yoke, there was a mechanical failure. The heavy aircraft could neither gain enough altitude to achieve lift nor slow down enough before it ran out of runway and slammed into a short retaining wall. Two crew members seated in the nose were killed. Eugene and the other ten men aboard were mostly unhurt.

Though an official inquiry absolved him of any responsibility, the mechanical failure and the death of two comrades haunted Eugene. He was reassigned to the States, where he served out his military career as a plane crash investigator.

During this second portion of his Army career, he was involved in a *second* crash, this time as a passenger. Again, he walked away from it. Soon after, he also walked away from the Army.

For his service in the military, Eugene was decorated with the Distinguished Flying Cross and the Air Medal. He retired with the rank of captain.

After the war, Eugene became a commercial airline pilot with Pan American World Airways, the country's largest air carrier at the time. Though still a young man, Pam Am often assigned him to their two longest routes, flying passengers from New York all the way to either Johannesburg, South Africa, or Calcutta, India.

On June 18, 1947, Eugene was aboard Pan Am Flight 121 from Calcutta back to New York. Since he had flown the plane to India, he was repositioned from flight crew to a passenger during the ride home. Five hours after takeoff

The New Addiction Treatment. David A. Patterson Silver Wolf, Oxford University Press. © Oxford University Press 2021. DOI: 10.1093/oso/9780197601372.003.0012

on the leg of the flight between Karachi, Pakistan, and Istanbul, Turkey, one of the Lockheed L-049 Constellation's four engines stopped working. It was Engine 1, on the left wing.

The plane's captain, Joseph Hart, remained calm. Even if he found a place to land immediately, there would be no way to get the engine repaired, so he decided to make the trip to Istanbul with his three spinning propellers. He reduced power and altitude, but even with these measures, the other engines began to run hot.

The pilot still had good reason to believe he could make it all the way to Istanbul, but things did not go his way. Without warning, Engine 2, also on the left wing, burst into flames. Captain Hart, now with two failed engines on the left side, knew he was not going to make it to Istanbul, and he began a rapid descent toward the desert below. He knew he was going to have to attempt a controlled, wheels-up, crash landing. One can only imagine what Eugene was thinking as the desert sand and Euphrates River grew large in his window, on this, his third time aboard an airplane headed for a hard impact with the earth.

Considering that Captain Hart was doing something he had never trained for (these were the days before flight simulators), he did as well as anyone could have hoped. Unfortunately, there was no margin for error and he did not thread the needle perfectly.

The left wing tip hit the hard-packed desert sand first, followed by the propeller on Engine 1, and then the body of the left wing. The impact tore the left wing from the fuselage of the plane, which hit hard on its belly with a violent thud. Sliding across the sand, the plane swung hard around to the left, turned 180 degrees and slid backward some 400 feet as it split in two. And then it caught fire.

As soon as the aircraft came to rest, two flight attendants and Eugene, who had suffered only two or three broken ribs, began evacuating passengers as quickly as they could.

One passenger, the Indian royal maharani of Pheleton, was trapped in the burning fuselage by her seat belt, hysterically thrashing around. Eugene calmed her down, forced the seat belt open, and helped her evacuate the wreckage. Eugene continued pulling passengers free until the wind suddenly shifted and blew fuel into the passenger seating area, creating an impenetrable inferno.

He could not save everyone, but thanks to Eugene and the two flight attendants, nineteen passengers survived the crash.

It is reasonable to assume that surviving three crashes was enough flying for Eugene Roddenberry. Indeed, just 11 months after the plane went down in the desert, he resigned from Pan Am. Nevertheless, it is equally likely that Eugene left Pan Am because he wanted to pursue his other passion: writing.

During both his military and civilian aviation careers, Eugene had penned many short stories and had several published.

Television was brand new in the late 1940s. There was very little programming, and it was tough to sell scripts. But Eugene was nothing if not persistent, and eventually he sold a few freelance scripts for shows like *Highway Patrol* and *Have Gun—Will Travel* and, as he became a known commodity, he focused on the genre he most loved, science fiction. Eugene created a TV series that, improbably, he sold to NBC.

On September 8, 1966, the first episode of Gene Roddenberry's show, *Star Trek*, aired on television. Though it ran for only three seasons, *Star Trek* spawned feature films, several popular spinoffs that continue to this day, and legions of fans. Many of whom were big thinkers and self-described nerds: people like Marty Cooper.

The brick

Marty Cooper was probably born to be an inventor. He once said that he was not that great of an engineer, but he was a good dreamer.

Born and bred in Chicago, Marty graduated from the Illinois Institute of Technology (IIT) with a bachelor's degree in 1950. He served as a submarine officer during the Korean conflict, returned to Chicago and, in 1957, went back to IIT and earned a master's degree in electrical engineering.

Any newly minted, young electrical engineer back in the late 1950s who wanted to stay in Chicago would probably do what Marty did: apply to Motorola. Chicago (and everyplace else) was not exactly Silicon Valley back then, and Motorola was just about the only tech company headquartered there.

Marty found a home at Motorola, and by the early 1970s he was working on the emerging science of mobile communications. It was a good fit because Marty saw the world and the people in it as being inherently mobile. Humans, while not necessarily nomadic, move around. Given a choice, most people would never choose to be tethered to their desks, homes, or offices. So

Marty's goal was to develop a communications product that could be used by people who were *on the move*.

At that time, telecommunications was dominated by AT&T. The telephone, which had a rotary dial, was wired to the wall, and you could go only as far away from the phone as its cord allowed. You could not even buy the thing; AT&T made their customers rent it. AT&T and their innovation hub, Bell Labs, had developed crude cellular technology, but their first car phones weighed more than 30 pounds and were terribly unreliable.

As Marty sat stewing about how he could fulfill his vision of bringing personal, portable communications to the world, he remembered how impressed he was, just a few years earlier, when he had watched those three seasons of *Star Trek*. Whenever Captain Kirk was beamed down to a planet or other location, he employed twenty-third-century technology to communicate with his crew orbiting above on the starship *Enterprise*. Kirk had a personal, mobile communicator, sort of *flip phone*, that did not require him to dial a number or have a corded connection. The starship captain pulled out his phone, flipped it open, and was immediately connected to his ship and crew.

Marty dreamed of a world where everyone would have their own personal phone number and their own personal phone. He wanted to create *Star Trek*'s phone of the future, something that could be handheld, cordless, unconnected to a place, but connected directly to a person.

It took Marty just 90 days to assemble a team of engineers and develop a working prototype, the DynaTAC 8000x. It was pejoratively branded the *brick* or the *shoe* because it was nearly a foot long and weighed about 2½ pounds. That is more than seven times heavier than a new iPhone, and, for that matter, it was straight up heavier than most shoes. This beast of a phone required a 10-hour charge to generate only 20 minutes of talk time. Marty said that did not matter because "a person couldn't hold it any longer than that."

It was unwieldy and limited by a short battery life. But it worked.

To show the world what he had finally created, Marty arranged a public relations stunt; an interview with a journalist and a photographer to capture the events as they unfolded. Walking down Sixth Avenue in Manhattan, he dialed the number of his main competitor at AT&T, Joel Engel.

In a stroke of good luck for Motorola, Joel answered. Marty said, "Joel, this is Marty. I'm calling you from a cell phone, a real handheld portable cell phone."

It was a long way from Alexander Graham Bell's first call, in which he said, "Mr. Watson, come here, I want you." The first-ever handheld cell phone conversation was, essentially, one man taunting his rival.

It took another 10 years before Motorola finally brought it to market, but Marty Cooper, who is regarded as the "father of the cell phone," was inspired by and will always be connected to Gene Roddenberry's vision of the future.

The twenty-third-century solution to solving our addiction treatment problem is most likely already in your pocket or pocketbook

One of the reasons I have begun each chapter with a story is because it is the way I was taught when I was young. The people who raised me were storytellers.

So when it comes to learning and teaching, my first instinct is to reach back for a story. It is a trait I come by honestly, something I inherited from my grandfather, though I will be the first to admit that, as a child, I could find him and his stories confounding. He would respond to my questions or concerns with tales of animals or spirits, and, when I was very small, I did not get the point—until, one day, I did.

I was in elementary school, maybe second grade, and I told my grandfather about a neighborhood bully—a kid I had thought was my friend—who had been spreading lies about our family.

My grandfather told me to come closer, and when I approached, he hoisted me up, sat me on his lap, and told me a story about a frog and a scorpion.

A scorpion needs to get from one side of a pond to the other, so when a frog comes by, the scorpion asks the frog to ferry him across. The frog demurs, saying, "No, if I carry you on my back, you'll sting me." The scorpion assures the frog that he will not do that. The frog agrees and allows the scorpion on his back for the ride across the pond. When the frog deposits the scorpion safely on the other side, the scorpion stings the frog. Before he dies, the frog cries, "How could you do that? You said you wouldn't sting me." The scorpion says, "What did you expect? I'm a scorpion; it is my nature to sting frogs."

It is an old parable, and to my great chagrin, I learned much later that my grandfather did not make it up himself.

At first, I did not have a clue about why my grandfather was telling this story. I wanted help with a bully, and all I was hearing was another fairy tale with a very unhappy ending. However, he then circled back around to the nature of bullies and how I should be aware and respond to their natures. For once, it all made sense and was permanently imprinted into my mind.

And from then on, I looked forward to speaking with him and hearing him spin these entertaining and beneficial yarns. I considered my grandfather a great teacher, and it was he who showed me the power of using a story to help open a mind before making a point or constructing an argument.

But the other reason to begin with these stories is that they show how the challenges we face in the treatment of addiction are neither unique nor insurmountable. Alternatively, it is to demonstrate that occasionally ordinary people do extraordinary things. Though it is hard to predict who is going to change the world, it is inspiring to be reminded that sometimes, out of nowhere or nothing, regular folks do exactly that.

Even though most of us will never achieve fame, infamy, or historical significance, we can still aspire to greatness. We can, and arguably should, try to be great at whatever endeavor—no matter how big or small—we choose.

However, many of us do not spend time thinking about how to be great. Most of us do not spend time thinking about being, well, anything. We just find a familiar routine in which familiar behaviors result in familiar rewards that keep us inside a familiar comfort zone.

Most of us continue repeating the same behaviors over and over again. Things were done a certain way before, and they become ingrained, reflexive. Yesterday, my grandfather taught me with stories. Today, I teach with stories. It is not a bad thing; it is just one example of how behaviors get hardwired and difficult to modify. It is as if deep-seated beliefs and behaviors become part of our DNA—immutable.

I have said previously in this book, and it is a mantra I repeat to my graduate students: *Behavior change is hard.* It is hard to change our own behaviors, and it is extremely hard to help others change theirs.

Unlike Gene Roddenberry or Marty Cooper, most of us do not have a vision of the future. A few of us do have a future vision, but lack the wherewithal to make it come true. If you have been around someone like this you know that a future vision without the will to make it real is just some person's opinion. It is often little more than the utopian dreaming or boozy finger-wagging that comes from shared bongs or adjoining bar stools.

I have a vision of the future of addiction treatment. It is simple, achievable, and modest. I do not dream of rainbows and daffodils, but I do dream of this: *addiction treatment that achieves a 5-year sustained recovery rate of 80 percent.*

Achieving this dream would require broad disruption and transformation in a field that has been in a poor-performing comfort zone and has not seen much innovation for the better part of a century. Achieving this dream would require massive changes in professional beliefs, practices, and institutions.

There are some who might argue that the American treatment industry is too big and too set in its ways to alter or at least alter anytime *soon*. Even if there were an earnest effort to achieve this grand vision, it would take years, if not decades, to turn this massive ship around and bring about the kinds of changes I am about to propose.

Moreover, if you made that argument almost any time before March 2020, you would have had a strong case. But in first 10 or 20 days of the third month in 2020, everything went up for grabs.

As I type this chapter, like all the others before, I am sitting in my university campus office. The space where I write has not changed; however, the hall outside my office and the campus outside my window have been transformed.

It is a week past the end of our school's scheduled spring break. Parking should be in short supply. Students, staff, and faculty should be shuffling between buildings, huddling inside classrooms, attending meetings in conference rooms, and socializing in cafes, salons, and green spaces.

Today, I pulled into an empty parking lot and walked across a desolate quadrangle toward my office. Sparrows, swallows, and robins were chirping and singing. Though the spring air was crisp and full of signs of life, like the abundant white and pink Alexandrina Saucer magnolias, humans were not.

Students were told to go home and not to return to the university after spring break. Their belongings are currently being packed up and shipped back to their family residences. All classes, meetings, and other activities that used to be done in person will occur now from the safety of cyberspace. All across America and the world, human activities and decisions have been disrupted. Professional, collegiate, and even high school sports seasons have been interrupted; concert tours have been suspended; live theaters and movie theaters have been closed; factories have been shuttered; restaurants are open only for delivery or takeout until they close permanently from lack of business; schools, businesses, friends, and family are turning to online, virtual interactions.

Our entire world was turned upside down in a matter of weeks by a ridiculously tiny and primitive life form: a strand of RNA with a genome so simple that its mere 30,000 pieces were mapped within weeks of being identified. But it is a pathogen sufficiently contagious and deadly that the disease it causes, COVID-19, spread around the planet and across our country at an exponential rate, overwhelming hospitals and our government's ability to stop it, with the potential of killing millions of people worldwide. The only way to prevent millions more from dying is to impose strict "social distancing," to keep people away from each other enough to flatten the curve of the infection rate from the virus.

The outpatient addiction clinic where I spend some of my time has suspended all in-person counseling. They—and all programs across the country like it—have begun offering all of their individual counseling services by phone and their group sessions by teleconferencing.

For the first time ever, funders have agreed to reimburse for these teleservices. Further, and even more surprising, compliance with HIPAA (Health Insurance Portability and Accountability Act) has been loosened. If patients do not have ready access to HIPPA-compliant technology, they can still receive services. It was agreed that continued therapeutic engagement during these unprecedented times was more important than HIPAA protection. In addition, 42 CFR Part 2 regulations (which limit disclosure of SUD patient records) have also been suspended in order to facilitate remote/virtual treatment.

Within days, changes that would have been laughable and even unethical to suggest, were now standard operating procedure. Our treatment system changed more in a past week than it had over the past several decades.

However, when we figure out how to control COVID-19, which we will certainly do, I believe the addiction treatment systems will return to the pre-coronavirus default requirement that all services be delivered in person. It will be like a family emerging from an underground shelter after a hurricane, viewing their destroyed unreinforced home and saying, "Now that the wind has died down, let's rebuild the house exactly as it was."

Until the current COVID-19 crisis, not much had changed in the treatment industry since Bill Wilson was voluntarily committed to New York's Towns Hospital in 1933, which was 2 years before he met Dr. Bob and cofounded Alcoholics Anonymous. The protocols and practices of today's addiction treatment would very much resemble those that Bill W. received nearly 90 years ago.

From its beginnings, addiction treatment, like most other psychotherapies, was delivered face to face and in person, whether one on one or in therapy/ educational groups. People suffering from this illness were, as they are today, required to be treated on site, inside a hospital, clinics, or providers' offices. Then, as now, all but the most intractable cases received outpatient treatment, meaning that after one or more hours of face-to-face interactions inside a clinic, patients return to their homes and communities until their next scheduled therapy session, which, since virtually all clinics are closed on weekends, might be 72 hours away.

Keeping patients bound and connected to the treatment center ensures the patients' financial liability to the center because when a patient does not attend in person, the program is not reimbursed.

Treatment programs that are not supported by state or federal grant dollars have to make sure they are admitting enough new patients to attend in person and generate sufficient revenue to remain profitable. Not-for-profit, publicly funded programs do not have this worry because their waiting rooms and waiting lists are filled well beyond their capacity to serve the people asking for their help.

In this day and age, it seems reasonable to suggest that the need to receive services on site is more than a bit antiquated. In the 1970s, Marty Cooper envisioned an industry rooted in the belief that humans are fundamentally and inherently mobile. People move around and do not wish to be tied down to anything.

Given our comfort with or preference for mobility, it stands to reason that it remains with us, even when we seek treatment for addictions. Unfortunately, patients seeking treatment do not have the choice to be both mobile and in treatment. Treatment requires that they commit to being at a specific place, at a specific time, for a specific number of hours, days, or weeks—even though (and this is the rub) their sobriety and recovery are most severely challenged only after they walk away from the clinic.

This is a fundamental problem with addiction treatment. People have to be tied down not only inside a clinic, but also when they are away from that clinic; unbound and trying to recover in their own communities, our profession has no continuing, in-the-moment connections with them. Treatment professionals have no good ways of comprehending the full height of the hurdles, or of intervening to lower the hurdles whenever the patient is out of the building. Therapists are largely impotent when their patients are nomadic and living their "normal" lives. These are lives that can be filled with enabling friends, codependent lovers, and countless subtle and complex psychological cues that might lead to a relapse. These same environments might also contain boundary-setting friends, strong, independent, supportive lovers, and countless subtle and complex psychological cues that might sustain recovery.

Many research dollars have been spent trying to understand how people change *during* treatment. Scales and practices have been developed to measure change in health behaviors while the therapist and patients sit together in a counseling office. I confess that I am guilty of participating in some of those empirical efforts, which I now see as probably necessary but certainly insufficient.

Why?

The answer is because people suffering from addictions *do not recover inside clinics. They recover in the real world, in their own communities.*

This should be a divine principle worthy of repetition: *Real treatment and recovery happen only after the patient has left the clinic and is back in their community.*

Unfortunately, as of early 2020 we still had almost no insight or understanding about how people change when they are no longer directly in the thrall of their therapist or counselor.

Clinics, whether the most expensive, private, celebrity-filled spas or the cheapest, grimiest, publicly funded places, know very little about the positive or negative value of their services once their patients return home. Today's treatment centers provide little more than a robust—albeit low-paying—jobs program for newly minted social workers and other human services workers. They do not provide a system of proven, effective care that is constantly measured, monitored, and improved.

Plaintiff's witness

Imagine you own a clinic providing treatment for addictions, and after operating for 5 or 6 years, you are sued by the family of a patient who died from an opioid overdose soon after leaving your facility. The family is accusing you of delivering poor-quality care, and they allege that the death of their loved one is, at least in some part, your fault.

Would you defend yourself by parroting your employer's party line that, "Our facilities are world class, we hire the best workers, and we use evidence-based practices"? Would you try to convince the court that your clinic must provide high-quality services because you are accredited by the Commission on Accreditation of Rehabilitation Facilities (CARF)?

How well might these explanations hold up on cross-examination? Imagine that you must truthfully answer a series of questions coming from a well-prepared attorney while a jury of your peers listens intently:

"How many other patients have died after leaving your facility?"

"What percentage of your patients achieve sustained recovery after 3 years?"

"Your state's Physicians Health Program reports about an 80 percent sustained recovery rate after five years. Can you please explain why your program does not offer the same treatment as these successful, well-monitored programs?"

"Didn't these grieving parents deserve to have their daughter's illness treated in a way that results in an 80 percent chance at success instead of your methods, which do not even measure how well you're doing with patients *during* treatment, much less 3 days after patients leave your facility?"

Generally speaking, your truthful answers to these questions will be some variation of "I don't know."

If America's addiction treatment industry were on trial, it would be facing hard prison time or stiff fines as it would be hard to defend its actions. Saying "I don't know" to these kinds of questions generally results in the court or jury finding in favor of the plaintiff.

So, how do we actually transform our treatment industry into a system that achieves an 80 percent success rate? It will take four things.

The first is offering treatment that is guided by real-time performance tools, such as clinical dashboards.

Second, treatment has to allow people to obtain professional services anytime, even without being tied to a physical treatment facility.

Third, treatment has to include the family, community, and employers.

Fourth, addiction treatment must employ a chronic care model that follows patients for multiple years.

How do we get there?

The answer is surprisingly simple and straightforward.

Where to?

The solution adopts the visions of Gene Roddenberry and Marty Cooper. It does this by riding the big waves created by Apple, whose mission is to bring "the best user experience to its customers through its innovative hardware, software, and services," and Google, whose mission is to "organize the world's information and make it universally accessible and useful."

Technology, in other words, must be employed to transform service delivery and enable the field to realize a vision of addiction treatment that produces an 80 percent rate of recovery after 5 years. For decades, the industry has ignored and discounted the benefits of technologies at its own, but mostly at its patients', peril.

The first thing—Air traffic control

The most vital technology tool for our new treatment industry is having the equivalent of an air traffic control system. Professional therapists, along with other treatment staff members (e.g., community support specialists, employment professionals, and peer supporters), need a tool that can display where their patients have been, where they are in the present moment, and whether they are on or deviating from a prescribed recovery flight plan.

Because most treatment organizations use some kind of electronic health record system (I have said previously, therapists and treatment staff are already good at collecting lots of patient data), such a tool is relatively simple to create and implement, in part because professional behaviors related to data collection do not have to change (behavior change is hard; technological advancement is much easier).

Currently, in treatment centers all across the country, the first couple of hours with a patient is spent conducting a thorough biopsychosocial assessment. This results in a treatment plan.

Technology tools such as clinical dashboards can now make use of assessment data and present them to front-line therapists *in real time*. Rather than having data entombed in an expensive electronic health record data coffin, they can be continuously leveraged for clinical guidance.

A recent study[119] demonstrated that, for general healthcare services, dashboard use is associated with both improved patient care and improved overall health outcomes. Further, increased information automation in hospital-based care is associated with lower mortality rates, lower rates of complications, and lower overall costs.[120]

The continuing evolution of dashboards, which were first implemented in the business world,[121] has produced increasingly positive outcomes in a number of different fields, including medicine. While our own work here in St. Louis has shown positive results from the use of a clinical dashboard (Appendix K), there are still insufficient studies to determine their efficacy specifically in regard to the treatment of addictions.

But there are good reasons to believe they will provide similar results. Clinical dashboards provide pertinent patient information in a timely manner, thereby improving clinical decision-making and the overall quality of care.[122]

What data do we need to monitor?
What is on the dashboard?

In medicine, physicians know what to measure and monitor in order to treat most illnesses. For example, when a patient has Type 2 diabetes, the doctors might measure hemoglobin A_{1C} or glycosylated hemoglobin. A cancer patient will have blood drawn also, but the doctor might be looking for specific biomarkers, antibodies, or indications of an immune system response. Though the patients, the diseases, and the tests will vary, medical monitoring measures are designed and administered to provide indications of whether treatments are showing positive results or not; they offer continuous guidance and course corrections.

If monitoring suggests that a treatment is ineffective, dosages are tweaked or alternative approaches are considered. These clinical best practices are expected of medical professionals. Moreover, because doctors are held legally responsible when malpractice leads to injury or death, such continuous quality assurance benefits both the health of the patient and the price of the doctor's insurance premiums.

In collaboration with a team of programmers and community leaders, I developed a clinical dashboard for the treatment of substance use disorders. We conducted interviews and collected surveys from front-line addiction therapists to determine the most important performance data measures to monitor. We asked these therapists what we thought would be a simple question: "What are the top five factors indicating a patient is staying on a successful path to recovery?"

During treatment, there are numerous items to consider. A partial list might include attendance at twelve-step meetings, employment stability issues, various social and community engagement behaviors, alcohol and drug use (both frequency and amounts), craving levels, self-reported anger and depression, medications prescribed, adherence to prescribed medication, and so on. The list of key data points to be measured and monitored grew with each therapist interview.

It quickly became apparent that there was no consensus among the therapists we surveyed. There was no agreed-on top five indicators that rose to the top as the most important to be monitored and measured. Instead, there were more than thirty items that were *all* considered to be important.

Therefore, there is a great deal of variability in the sorts of things therapists are *trying* to measure and monitor. And what became clear was that the tool they relied on most frequently to guide and focus their attention to whatever variables they believed to be most important was intuition: their gut feeling about how their patient was doing.

Despite a lack of consensus among the therapists we interviewed or surveyed, there is a fair amount of literature, including and especially the Substance Abuse and Mental Health Services Administration's work on *the four dimensions of recovery*,[123] which identifies some indicators as more salient than others. With SAMHSA's findings in mind, our team developed a clinical dashboard that collects treatment and recovery data on what we consider to be the *vital signs of recovery*.

It is a standard operating procedure that before a person meets with their physician, a nurse first collects their vital signs. In a similar fashion, we taught therapists how to collect the vital signs of recovery data at the beginning of every individual counseling session with every patient entering their offices.

The therapist asks patients a series of quantitative questions. Though the interviews with front-line therapists yielded several dozen vital items, we knew that SAMHSA had gathered a team of national experts to work through and develop a much smaller list of four broad items—health, hope, purpose, and community[123]—and described in detail how each of these dimensions serves the goal of full recovery.

Our dashboard employs Likert scale questions to measure and monitor these four dimensions during standard outpatient treatment. The dashboard provides therapists real-time data to enable them to identify and intervene on low-scoring dimensions in order to increase those scores, as well as pointing out areas of strength that the therapist can validate and support. Capturing these data allows therapists to monitor their patients' recovery every day and to track measurable change over time (Appendix L).

Asking these questions at the beginning of each individual counseling session provides familiarity, structure, and a little less room for the therapist to be led astray by hunches or gut feelings. Most importantly, the collection and vigilant monitoring of these vital signs of recovery provide quantifiable performance data for the therapist. Therapists and patients alike can keep track of whether or not there is progress toward recovery.

While this effort is a new and exciting way to measure and motivate a patient's recovery, the larger aim is to help evaluate and improve the performance of therapists and to remind therapists and their supervisors that it is the *therapist's* responsibility to help their patients achieve and maintain sobriety.

Because the dashboard tool displays various patient characteristics (age, race, gender, diagnoses, etc.), it reveals how well each therapist performs with each type of patient. It might reveal that, for example, a therapist does best with African American women between the ages of 30 and 40, while another, who does poorly with this group, excels with transgender men over 50 who have co-occurring major depression.

Just as professional baseball players have their own chewing gum cards enumerating their career statistics, professional therapists will also have their own performance cards. Therapists can dispassionately evaluate their own performance, see how they do compared with intra-agency or national standards, work to improve weak areas, and/or play to their strengths.

Recall our previous discussion about patient–therapist matching. Not every therapist does well with every patient. The clinical dashboard shows these data in real time and makes it easier to assign patients to the therapist most likely to ensure recovery or at least achieve a discharge after *program completion with staff approval*, not the therapist who has the lowest caseload and first-available opening in their schedule.

A clinical director can monitor the entire clinic's aggregated scores as well as visualize individual therapist performance. When group and individual clinical supervision happens, if it does happen, skill development can be tailored and based on real data. Because all therapists should be working toward increasing patient retention, during clinical supervision sessions the important skill and proven retention intervention of building a therapeutic alliance, can be both honed and monitored for impact in real time. Further, when new interventions are deployed, expecting to influence a particular variable, a clinical dashboard tool can display immediate results.

The clinical dashboard provides something that's been absent: the equivalent of an air traffic control system that displays real-time patient performance data while treatment is actually happening inside clinics.

But what about Marty Cooper's belief that people are inherently mobile? How can we continue treatment and connectedness after patients return to their own communities?

The second thing

Imagine our national air traffic control system not having the ability to track aircraft in flight. Essentially, this is our treatment system. We know something about a patient's condition when they arrive, when we conduct an assessment, and when we see patients while they are inside clinics. But once they walk out the door for a day, a weekend, or longer, we—and they—are flying blind.

Mobile technology can help us bridge this enormous knowledge gap.

Cellular phones have come a long way since Marty Cooper's brick or AT&T's 30-pound car phones. Today, about 96 percent of Americans own a cell phone, and 85 percent of those are *smart*phones.[124]

This means that 85 percent of Americans are walking around with a treatment delivery system in their pockets. Smartphones will enable people to obtain professional services any time and anywhere without having to physically enter a treatment facility.

Our team developed smartphone tools that enable patients to recover in their own communities while providing critical data and performance graphs to their therapists' clinical dashboards. When patients return to the clinic, their therapists' interventions are informed by in-the-moment data, not after-the-fact, retrospective self-reports.

However, do patients really need to come back to a clinic to receive services?

Our smartphone app bundles a suite of technologies that untether treatment from treatment centers. Many features are still being tested for efficacy, but two established elements of our mobile app include *ecological momentary assessment* and *spatial geolocation*.

The best way to understand ecological momentary assessments (a phrase that flows so easily from the tongue it could only have been named by an academic) is by analogy:

In medicine, the old method for a physician to monitor the side effects of a newly prescribed drug was to prescribe a medication and then schedule a follow-up office visit a couple of weeks in the future. The patient and physician would reconvene, and the doctor would ask the patient to recall any issues or complaints with the new drug. Using those *recall data*, the doctor would make any necessary adjustments.

The new and more valid and reliable way to measure any medication's side effects is to use the patient's smartphone and regularly check in throughout the same 2-week period. The patient will be texted (either randomly or on a planned schedule) brief surveys about various side effects they might be experiencing and asked to immediately respond to those questions.

Repeated measurements over time within a patient's natural environments provide reliable and ecologically valid assessments compared to the usual, single retrospective assessment. These texted *check-in* (what I'm calling *ecological momentary*) assessments are increasingly used in healthcare. Their more precise and accurate measurements of subjective health-related issues are significant and proven.[125,126]

Having survey questions at the ready for mobile patients who are working on recovery from addiction in their own communities can begin to fill many performance gaps.

The Substance Abuse and Mental Health Services Administration's four dimensions of recovery work group and our own research would agree that recovery is positively associated with *internal social bonding* and *overcoming risk factors* in one's own community.[127] Having strong social bonds with families and communities decreases behaviors that lead to harmful substance use.[128] Patients without those bonds, living in deprived communities, have harmful substance use reinforced or even promoted.[129,130]

The success or failure of therapeutic behavior change is strongly related to the environment where that change is expected to occur.[131] The research suggests that in-the-moment patient assistance and some alternative behavioral options increase the likelihood of sustained recovery.[132]

This is something that is not debatable. We know that the chances of sustained, long-term recovery increase when patients are bonded with positive aids to sobriety in their own communities and their community-level threats are addressed.[133–135]

Speak with any person who is working toward recovery and has returned to substance use: The return was mostly initiated by in-the-moment, impulsive acts. Comments such as "I wasn't thinking" or "It just happened" are common. Believe these statements or not, relapse or the return to use happens a lot throughout our current treatment systems. It even happens inside highly successful physician health programs about 70 percent of the time.[136] Although the physician health program research article did not explicitly state this, it is most likely that these relapses happened once the physician transitioned from an inpatient residential facility to their own community and less-restrictive outpatient treatment. While their relapse prevention strategies (e.g., medical board oversight, urine screens, etc.) worked for the 30 percent, behavioral change was unsteady for the majority.

Having the ability to check in throughout their usual day with patients on important factors such as craving levels, mood (e.g., depression, anxiety), and other conditions that threaten recovery is possible with mobile technology. Further, having those assessment data circle back to the clinical dashboard enables professionals to more fully understand what is happening on the ground, out beyond the walls of the treatment center, as the patient tries to make their way in the world.

In addition to leveraging phones to check in with patients and assessing certain conditions in their natural environments, geolocation can be used to *intervene* and *modify* behavior. We can mark and define locations in a patient's communities as being either supportive (e.g., twelve-step meetings, recovering communities, houses of worship, etc.) or threatening (e.g., bars, liquor stores, drug use areas, etc.). When the patient and their phone cross these premapped fences, our check-in assessment surveys can be launched to gather important in-the-moment data. More importantly, we can instantly dispatch tailored interventions to interrupt potentially harmful behaviors and encourage helpful ones. Mobile technology, properly deployed, can actually influence intentions.[137–142]

The overall goal of the smartphone tool is to remind patients, in real time and within their own communities, of risky and protective locations. The app can reward patients in protective locations and alert them and possibly interrupt their thinking or redirect their attention if they find themselves approaching risky ones.

Additionally, the app sustains recovery by promoting internal bonding with positive supports, including their recovery support community.

All of these data—assessments, interventions, day and time entering and exiting locations, and so on—are fed back to the therapist's clinical dashboard. Some of these data are also available for patients to see on their phones, offering insights into obstacles, encouragement for progress toward recovery, and gentle deterrence from risk factors. Having the combination of *in-treatment* and *in-community* data increases the attention paid to a disease that tends to recur whenever surveillance is relaxed or insufficient.

A clinical dashboard that integrates the data that come from a patient's time inside of a treatment clinic with their time back in their community will better enable professional therapists to stay connected with, and achieve better outcomes for, the patients they serve.

In the fight against the cunning nature of addiction, a delay of hours, days, or even weeks could be fatal. We can now, digitally, help people monitor themselves and then send those data back to their therapist in real time. Change, and real improvement, is possible.

We here at Washington University's Brown School of Social Work, one of this country's top-ranked programs, responded to the COVID-19 pandemic by transforming a bricks-and-mortar building full of classrooms into a virtual graduate program in which all courses are delivered online to students who have left campus and in many cases left St. Louis and now reside all over the world. All faculty and staff meetings are held via Zoom or other teleconferencing platforms. The school still exists, but in a very different form, and this complete metamorphosis occurred in less than 10 days.

My healthcare insurance provider will now reimburse for telehealth services to deal with m of my medical needs. Here and across the country, patients are not sitting in waiting rooms or doctor's offices. Physicians are using widely available teleconferencing tools to interact with their patients, using a streaming broadband connection in lieu of face-to-face encounters. Adding these types of technology tools to the suite of services discussed above transports most critical treatment procedures into cyberspace.

Treatment clinics could begin to resemble air traffic control towers, with professionals stationed in front of computer screens interacting with their patients in real time, 24/7. Patients who have these tools on their phones can rest assured they will have a virtual safety net and a team of professionals ready to help at a moment's notice.

Moreover, maybe best of all, every one of these services would collect highly valuable recovery data, feeding them back to the professional, who can then deploy tailored interventions that are guided by performance data.

Being able to see real-time data and a patient's response to an intervention used, therapists, along with their clinical supervisors, will be better informed and better equipped to make any treatment plan adjustments.

The human piece

Let me be abundantly clear about something I have not yet said explicitly: Real therapists still need to establish real therapeutic alliances with real patients. This—not technology, not medications like buprenorphine, not even twelve-step meetings, the threat of job loss or financial ruin—is the most important piece of professionally assisted recovery.

The critical importance of the role of the human therapist, and the ability of the therapist to convey empathy, to earn trust, to establish rapport, and to inspire hope, cannot be overstated. The healing potency of real, human beings; trained, skilled therapists who know how to connect with patients and give them a reason to seek recovery and who also know when and how to deploy—and commit to delivering—evidence-based interventions, like motivational interviewing and cognitive behavioral therapy, cannot be stressed enough.

However, if and only if a human bond is forged, the need for ongoing face-to-face encounters begins to diminish and then the role of technology can expand. I am proposing technologies that *assist* treatment and expand its reach, I am not calling for technology to replace human-to-human encounters.

Treatment delivered by a well-programmed avatar is likely to be as unsuccessful as a human who is underprogrammed on empathy. The technology assists a human-to-human relationship and increases its horsepower so it might be more likely to bring about the desired but very difficult change.

Technologies cannot successfully replace human therapists, but they might replace the requirements of people having to be physically present and connected to clinics.

The third thing

Should we wish to engage with it, there is a robust, mature social networking infrastructure that is already an accepted part of our everyday lives.

The mobile tools our team developed include an option for patients to invite "their people" to be part of their support system. Patients can, if they wish, share their recovery journey with their family members, friends, twelve-step community members as well as a supportive employer.

The physician health programs consider the physician's community to be such an important part of recovery that their involvement in the treatment process is required. Here, with a bit less leverage, the best we can do is strongly encourage it.

A movement away from anonymity has been gaining traction in the past decade. While there are a lot of support groups and fellowship organizations that use *anonymous* as the second word in their two-word titles, and they continue to be vitally important in the lives of millions, remaining anonymous is not the only route to recovery.

In fact, to help erase the stigma that continues to surround this illness, there is much to be said about treating this disease as openly as we treat other chronic health conditions. We are not required to provide treatment for substance use disorders in darkness, inside of facilities that do not allow anyone but the patient to enter. Treatment facilities should be community gathering places. If this is a disease—an illness that requires professional services inside of a clinic—then families, friends, and communities should be surrounding the person who suffers from it. Just as when someone is admitted to a hospital, there should be accommodations for the sick person's natural support systems to be involved in the healing process. To deny this connection to those suffering from an addiction is at best unhelpful and, at worst, unconscionably cruel.

Our technology tools offer all of the opportunities and healing properties that come when a supportive community encircles a person suffering from an illness. The sooner this happens the better for patients.

Exposing our current treatment industry to the sunlight will also help disinfect stigma, increase the understanding of this illness, and improve the miserable, historical outcomes that persist throughout this system of care.

The last thing

The fourth and final condition that must be changed in order to offer a new and improved, 80 percent successful, recovery rate, is providing treatment services using the chronic care model rather than the current acute care model.

This shift would be made possible by again having access to a smartphone. When you travel with a mobile device, you travel with treatment.

Cybertreatment can continue as long as needed. There are no reasons to "graduate" from anything. Just as physician health programs continue monitoring and provide services for a full 5 years, so too can cybertreatment go on for as long as it is needed.

Addiction treatment can continuously be delivered over time with varying levels of intensity, rather than the usual stopping and starting process that ceases every 28 days or so and resumes (if the patient has access to care) at every new relapse.

In a mobile-based program, patients feeling the need to reach out to professionals and engage the cybersafety net tools can easily and instantly select from a menu of recovery support options such as what was previously discussed as well as mobile telehealth. Patients needing to speak with a therapist or community support specialist can pull out their phone and use it like Captain Kirk connecting with his crew. Services can be at the ready whenever and wherever someone needs them.

One of the most fatal flaws in the current addiction treatment industry is ending the treatment too soon. The standard operating procedure is to hand off the remaining treatment responsibilities to twelve-step programs that are, by design, unprofessional in nature. It is the equivalent of ending cancer treatments after one fifth of the remedy has been provided and then suggesting that the remaining treatment be obtained solely from a group of cancer survivors.

Just like Cancer Anonymous is a fellowship of people with cancer sharing their *experience, strength, and hope with each other so that they may solve their common problem and help others,* so are all the other twelve-step fellowship programs.

Our much needed and important twelve-step fellowship programs support people *during and after* treatment; they are not the providers of treatment.

Being dependent on the good folks in the twelve-step fellowship to *take over* the treatment of patients discharged from treatment is no longer required. With a smartphone in every pocket or pocketbook, professional service providers and supportive communities are a click away.

Bringing on the future

Currently, a reimbursement model for cybersupported treatment does not exist. While radical temporary changes brought about by the COVID-19 pandemic might someday lead to permanent policy changes, it is far more likely that insurance companies and state funders will resist and refuse paying for these still nontraditional services. Empirical investigations and the evidence they generate can speed things up, but the most likely way forward is to first offer these new treatment services to individuals who can afford to pay for them.

It is ironic, in a way, because in medicine, experimention and innovation quite often come first to the poorest patients. Doctors in training hone their skills on the uninsured; clinical trials are conducted on those who cannot afford traditional services or find themselves in the most desperate straits. But in this instance, the "guinea pigs" will be the people who have financial means to pay out of pocket.

There is a large cohort of Americans who would happily, if given the choice, opt for cybertreatment services rather than enter into the hidden, off-the-beaten path clinic locations. Implemented fully, it would provide the most up-to-date services using real data to guide services.

With so many addiction treatment facilities charging high fees to deliver the current short-term, gut feeling, lousy-outcome model of care, there is little risk to the early adopters.

Unfortunately, those who are in most need of these high-quality, data-guided services are unlikely to get them. Despite the availability and efficacy of mobile treatment tools, the vast majority of existing treatment providers do not use them and are unlikely to adopt them. Some clinics lack technological knowledge and resources to customize off-the-shelf apps. While there are myriad types of recovery apps already on the market and available for wide use, there is no accepted interfacing tool—like an air traffic control system—that will collect and synchronize data into an actionable treatment guide.

In addition, of course, other reasons range from a lack of capacity for managing and synthesizing the large volume of patient data generated by mobile apps, to institutional dogma and resistance to change. The main argument for creating a new treatment system that fully leverages technology, rather than recommending that the current system simply augment its current services with technology tools, is that there are too many institutional obstacles and too much internal resistance to change.

It is probably the same reason Uber did not collaborate with the taxicab industry. Uber just went its own way and did its own thing, and Uber certainly disrupted the way people pay for transportation and who does the driving.

Imagine a treatment system that begins with someone from the comfort of their home completing an online biopsychosocial–spiritual assessment along with a few other assessments to measure recovery capital and the four dimensions of recovery (home, health, community, and purpose). Within 30 minutes, a link is sent, and mobile application products are downloaded and installed on the new patient's phone.

Downloading an app notifies a therapist to contact the patient to arrange for an initial meeting—in person at a clinic or via telehealth if the patient prefers—where assessments and diagnoses are discussed and where a therapeutic alliance begins.

The therapist has been matched with the patient using data from the biopsychosocial assessment in order to maximize the likelihood of forming a strong relationship quickly.

In early sessions, the therapist and patient identify community locations that are protective and those that pose risks. Family, friends, and other community supporters are identified and entered into the system, and these connections grow and are adjusted as the patient travels the recovery path. Professional community support specialists, peer supporters, and employment consultants are integrated into the recovery plan.

Depending on the severity of the disorder and any potential employment conditions or criminal justice involvement, the system can offer some accountability tools. In physician health programs, state medical boards insist on random urine screens. This system can offer random prompts for drug screens and other products (e.g., photographs of pupil dilation/constriction or "roadside sobriety tests" using the smartphone's gyroscope or wearable sensors to record a patient's ability to walk a straight line) that can be leveraged in the moment. Incorporating these tools into physician health programs and those needing higher levels of oversight will further ensure the public's safety.

Recall the marine who told me that our military understands how to project its resources, in which order, onto its enemies, and recall Joe McQuany's observation that treatment is a sequence of events that leads to a conclusion. In the new addiction treatment, data analysis will allocate specific resources to specific patients. Data analysis will yield a specific sequence of events—customized for each patient—leading to a positive conclusion.

Partnerships

For this (or any) new treatment system to become established, academic–community partnerships will be vitally important.

This proposed system will generate a great deal of data, and having researchers and academics available to analyze these data will guide practice and ensure that improvements are continuously incorporated back into the system.

For instance, it will be important to understand which therapist factors (e.g., general demographics, personality traits) are associated with patient success. We would want to investigate whether the usual activities offered in treatment, such as educational and therapeutic groups, can be equally or more effective if delivered in a more tailored manner. We would want to know if the therapeutic alliance and other counseling skills could be improved by monitoring therapist's scorecards and targeted clinical supervision.

There are a number of other research and practice opportunities that would result from the wide use of cyber-, mobile, smart-phone treatment. Large data sets would enable prediction models that could generate treatments customized for a patient's unique profile. Data-generated findings would direct interventions, in a sequential manner, in order to mitigate addiction's pull and support patients' protective assets. With these real-world data, researchers and practitioners would be able to run predictive analytics, "war games," to model various treatment intervention deployment scenarios in order to find those that will work best.

Dr. Anthony Fauci, director of the National Institute of Allergy and Infectious Diseases, repeatedly said, "I think we should be overly aggressive [with COVID-19] and get criticized for overreacting."

The same is true for substance use disorders. Though at this point, it would be impossible to overreact. In 2017, there were 47,600 Americans who died from a drug overdose. No one was criticized for overreacting.

In 2018, there were 67,000 Americans who died from a drug overdose. I do not recall much of an overreaction.

To stop the spread of the novel coronavirus and COVID-19 we have shut down our cities; eliminated all international and most domestic travel;

temporarily banned all forms of public gatherings, including weddings, funerals, and religious services; endured weeks of social distancing; and injected trillions of dollars into our economy. To try to prevent sick patients from overwhelming our healthcare system as it did in Italy and Spain, our federal government has (clumsily and belatedly) put itself on a war footing to address the threat. This includes measures like deploying the Army Corps of Engineers to construct field hospitals in under a week, sending huge hospital ships—converted supertankers, each with a thousand patient rooms and a dozen operating theaters—to ports in New York and Los Angeles harbors, while, in the absence of a comprehensive, cohesive, organized federal response, the hardest hit states scrambled to find additional protective personal equipment (e.g., masks, face shields, gloves, and gowns) for the front-line healthcare providers and ventilators to keep the most critically ill patients alive.

Much of this is absolutely necessary and, arguably, too little. To stop the spread of this virus, other countries have responded earlier, with far more draconian measures. The highly contagious and sometimes fatal disease disrupted our lives to an almost unimaginable extent. It put an end to "business as usual."

Too many of our children, parents, siblings, and friends have died from problems related to alcohol and other drugs. It is past time for a disruption in the addiction treatment system. Given the lamentable failure rate in this illness's treatment, it is time to put an end to business as usual and try something new.

Concluding Thoughts

The famed journalist and satirist H. L. Mencken (1880-1956) said: "For every complex problem, there is an answer that is clear, simple, *and wrong.*"

My proposed disruption to the way we currently treat addiction could very well be another in a long line of solutions that sounds neat and plausible but may, for a variety of reasons, still be wrong. From using heroin as a cure for morphine-addicted Civil War veterans to throwing drunkards in the hoosegow back in the Old West, history is replete with wrong answers that made sense at the time.

But given the size and scope of the problem, there must be something better than (once again) treating opioid use disorder with opioids and (still) treating alcohol use disorder with little more than prayer and fellowship.

As we have seen throughout this book: In virtually all other areas of public safety, people and professions learn from their mistakes.

Every airline crash is investigated, and lessons are learned to avoid future mishaps. This is true for all types of public transportation, including amusement park rides.

Doctors use checklists and evidence-based medicine to prevent bad outcomes and improve the chances of recovery while minimizing complications.

But for more than a century, the treatment of addiction has been relegated to a peculiar netherworld, caught somewhere between mental health, neuroscience, and willful, sinful, self-induced behavior that's no one's fault besides the sufferer's.

Failure is tolerated in the world of addiction treatment to a degree that is quite literally unimaginable in any other area of science or medicine.

Unfortunately, given the lack of funding for both research and treatment, there remains a dearth of effective, high-quality, evidence-based specialized care. What *is* available tends to be either terribly expensive or hopelessly overcrowded. In addition, both factors—expense and lack of capacity—limit access, which means treatment failures will persist.

The New Addiction Treatment. David A. Patterson Silver Wolf, Oxford University Press. © Oxford University Press 2021. DOI: 10.1093/oso/9780197601372.003.0013

The ideas proposed here aim to make treatment more available, to more people, more often, for a much longer period of time. It proposes a cost-effective means of converting our acute care model of addiction treatment into a chronic care model that can offer ongoing support, services, and interventions over many years. The use of mobile technology is in no way a panacea, but it will extend the reach of treatment centers so more sufferers can be served and so more will stay connected to treatment. It will lower the cost of helping people, making treatment more accessible. And it will make it possible to stay in close contact with our patients for years instead of days or weeks.

We have to do things differently. Someone has to scream from the rooftops that our friends and family are dying in great numbers while our profession plods along or stands idly by, employing but not improving the same tired, shopworn, ineffective methods.

Addiction is a chronic, recurring brain disease. As far as we know, it's incurable. But as far as we also know, it's very, very treatable.

Unfortunately, only a very select group of Americans are provided care that reaches an 80 percent 5-year recovery rate. Further unfortunate news is that because of our antiquated system, the new addiction treatment proposed here might only be available to those who can afford it. But when insurance providers and state funders realize that this new treatment is grounded in real data, real outcome performance measures, and is both effective and cost-effective, they might be willing to support it for everyone.

We know the methods and technologies to improve care can be folded into standard treatment models. The science tells us that performance-based practices will improve patient care.

Change, in other words, is possible.

Too many people have been thrown off too many roller coasters for too long. Too many people have not reached their planned destinations during flights. And for far too long, too many people have been provided bloodletting treatments without any outcome performance measures.

We know how to successfully treat people who are suffering from this well-known disease—if only we have the will to learn from our mistakes and the audacity to try something new.

Acknowledgments

I could not have written this, or any other book, without the help and guidance of Ron and Pat McKiernan; two guys who, when I met them more than thirty years ago, provided nothing but, as the song goes, amazing grace. They both worked hard to "save a wretch like me." They set me on a path towards—and were in no small part architects of—my recovery from addiction.

Mike Morrison has been a dear personal friend and thought partner to me. More than that, I consider him a brother.

Howard Weissman has been a great friend, ruthless editor, organizer of my crackpot ideas and sometimes a wordsmith.

Dean Mary McKay at Washington University in St. Louis' Brown School of Social Work has been a constant supporter. She gave me the freedom to pursue my research interests and express my views, even when they were iconoclastic. I consider her and all of my Brown School colleagues as dear friends. I also want to thank all of them for honoring me by starting the David Patterson Silver Wolf Scholarship. The scholarship will support future generations of social workers who will, I trust, employ evidence-based practices.

Dr. Catherine Dulmus, Director of the Buffalo Center for Social Research at the University at Buffalo, began as an academic advisor. She taught me the skills necessary to become a high-quality researcher. She also became a close friend of our family.

I'd also like to express my appreciation to production editor Poonguzhali Ramasamy and Dana Bliss, executive editor at Oxford University Press. Upon learning of my health challenges, they both worked long hours to accelerate the publication of this book.

Finally, to my beloved wife Nikki. I owe her everything. She and our three children, Ambra, Conall and Aidan have been and will always be: My Love. My Life. My Everything.

HOW BIG IS BIG?

Appendix A

In the National Institute of Drug Abuse's Trends & Statistics webpage (https://www.drugabuse.gov/related-topics/trends-statistics), lots of data are provided on the amount of drug use that is occurring throughout the United States. The below table indicates that the costs to our nation that are directly related to the abuse of tobacco, alcohol, and illicit drugs is approximately $740 billion annually.

Costs of Substance Abuse

Abuse of tobacco, alcohol, and illicit drugs is costly to our Nation, exacting more than $740 billion annually in costs related to crime, lost work productivity and health care.[**]

	Health Care	Overall	Year Estimate Based On
Tobacco[1,2]	$168 billion	$300 billion	2010
Alcohol[1,3]	$27 billion	$249 billion	2010
Illicit Drugs[4,5]	$11 billion	$193 billion	2017
Prescription Opioids[6]	$26 billion	$78.5 billion	2013

Appendix B

On the National Institute of Drug Abuse Nationwide Trends page (https://www.drugabuse.gov/publications/drugfacts/nationwide-trends), it shows an estimated 24.6 million Americans aged 12 and older, almost 10 percent of the population, used an illicit drug in the past month in 2013. While most drugs of use have remained the same over time, two substances, marijuana and illicit drugs, have steadily increased over time.

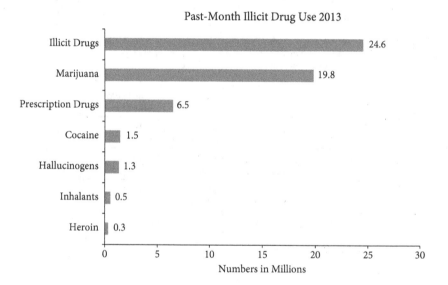

Past-Month Illicit Drug Use 2013

Numbers in Millions

Appendix C

The March 24, 2017, *Washington Post* article "The Disease Killing White Americans Goes Way Deeper Than Opioids" by Jeff Guo (https://www.washingtonpost.com/news/wonk/wp/2017/03/24/the-disease-killing-white-americans-goes-way-deeper-than-opioids/), it discusses the work of Princeton scientists Anne Case and Angus Deaton and highlights the three issues causing the "disease of despair": drugs, alcohol, and suicide.

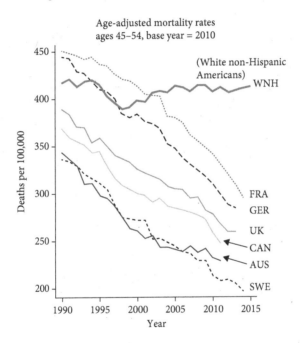

In the above graph that comes from Case and Deaton's study and inserted into the 2017 *Washington Post* article shows that while other first-world countries have experienced significant decreases in deaths, America's death rates, since 1995, has been the outlier, increasing over time.

The *Washington Post* continues to write about this problem as it continues to worsen. In a November 30, 2018, published article, "America Is Losing Ground to the Death and Despair," life expectancy fell again for this specific, non-Hispanic White population. The "surge" in drugs and suicide is listed as the reason for this outcome.

A year later, on November 26, 2019, another article was posted, "'There's Something Terribly Wrong': Americans Are Dying Young at Alarming Rates" (https://www.washingtonpost.com/health/theres-something-terribly-wrong-americans-are-dying-young-at-alarming-rates/2019/11/25/d88b28ec-0d6a-11ea-8397-a955cd542d00_story.html). Joel Achenbach's article once again discusses the high mortality rates for Americans between the ages of 25 and 64. While these Americans would be considered being in the "prime of their lives" because they live in America and not in another wealthy nation, their lives have been cut short by the disease of despair.

Appendix D

During my work with the Community Academic Partnership on Addiction (CAPA), we surveyed 400 front-line substance use order therapists. We used several established scales as well as developed some of our own questions to understand what was happening on the front lines of treatment. The table below is the result of asking therapists to name and rank their top three evidence-based interventions (CBT, cognitive behavioral therapy; MI, motivational interviewing) used during their usual, everyday services.

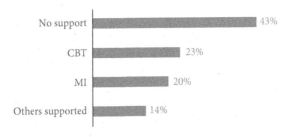

Are front-line substance use disorder therapists
using practices supported by science?

As indicated, the most interventions listed as being top ranked were not empirically supported. Asking over 400 therapists to list three items resulted in more than 1,200 possibilities. It took the research team to process these options and validate whether they were, in fact, not supported by science. We learned various names of "interventions" that were being deployed in addiction treatment facilities.

Many of the supposed interventions listed were not interventions at all but mostly models, concepts, or frameworks of therapy. For instance, many therapists listed "solution focused" as their top regular practice, just to name one. While some would strongly argue that this "therapy" is an empirically supported intervention, we found no support for that position.

How we arrived at these decisions was reviewing the scientific literature looking for random controlled trials, placebo trials, systematic reviews, and so on. It was not our team who decided, but literature. This is part of the problem throughout the treatment industry in both specialized addiction services and behavioral health services in general. Therapists are free to use the therapies of their own choice, regardless if those interventions held up in multiple peer-reviewed clinical trials with the results published in our accepted scientific journals.

Dr. Bruce Thyer has written about this issue,[1,2] and in his recent book *Science and Pseudoscience in Social Work Practice*,[3] Dr. Thyer and his coauthor outlined the rules and conditions of determining what are and are not scientific-supported practices, along with how to evaluate these practices. It should be required reading for all students who are entering the behavioral treatment field.

1. Pignotti M, Thyer BA. Use of novel unsupported and empirically supported therapies by licensed clinical social workers: An exploratory study. *Soc Work Res.* 2009;33(1):5–17.

2. Thyer BA, Myers LL. The quest for evidence-based practice: A view from the United States. *J Soc Work.* 2011;11:8–25.

3. Thyer B, Pignotti M. *Science and Pseudoscience in Social Work Practice.* New York: Springer; 2015.

Appendix E

A scale that the 400 plus therapists completed was Arron's Evidence-Based Practice Attitude Scale (EBPAS). As a reminder, part of the questions in the EBPAS focused on the likelihood that a therapist would adopt a new evidence-based intervention if that intervention was required by a superior. The survey specifically targets the question as it relates to three superiors, asking how likely they would adopt the new intervention if it were required by their supervisor, agency, or state.

Therapists who would **not** use a new EBP if it was required by...

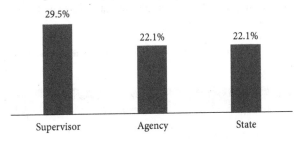

As the above table shows, almost one third of the therapists would not adopt a new intervention (EBP, evidence-based practice) if their supervisor required it. While the percentage of therapists dropped by seven when it was their agency or state requiring the adoption of a new intervention, a solid 22 percent still reported they would not comply with an agency or state requirement.

This should be concerning for patients entering treatment facilities and their families expecting high-quality, empirically supported care. It should also be concerning for organizations whose employees would be so willing to disregard the mandates of using new practices that are supported by science.

Appendix F

What might explain this troubling hard stance by therapists is EBPAS's other questions related to the therapist's own practice value system. For instance, a question asks what is more useful, interventions supported by research (science) or clinical experience (practice wisdom).

The graph below shows that almost 27 percent of front-line therapists valued their own practice wisdom over science. It is important to know that these therapists were working without any real-time or historical data measures. For instance, they would not be able to produce any document or report showing their past practice performance results. Like others, they were dealing with high caseloads and guided by good intentions and bad intuitions.

Practice wisdom is more important than new science?

Appendix G

Below are the pictures Bill Miller displayed at his presentation during a 2015 conference sponsored by CAPA and addiction organizations in St. Louis, Missouri. Dr. Miller explained the power of empathy and how humans notice and evaluate several cues sometimes without overtly trying.

Appendix H

Below is the table that shattered my hypothesis that patient–therapist matching matters. In order for my hypothesis to be supported, the non-White female match should have resulted in the highest percentage of success. As my yellow highlights reveal, it was the White male therapist who had superior success outcomes. Considering just the female-to-female match, which had the highest total sample ($n = 94 + 52$), those single-digit outcomes are concerning. It should raise questions regarding the practices and benefits of female gender matching. The other concerning factor of this study was the lack of non-White male therapists having no non-White female patients in their caseloads.

While it is a common practice to conduct gender-specific treatment, mostly female-to-female individual and group matching, in this study, White male therapists did at least have ten female patients in their caseloads. You will also notice in the full table in Appendix I non-White male therapists also had no White female patients.

Again, while this is one study, because we do not have these types of performance data widely available for evaluation, it is not known whether non-White male therapists are commonly not matched throughout treatment organizations with female patients or not.

Therapist race and gender	Patient race and gender	N	Success
White male	Non-White female	10	40.0%
Non-White female	Non-White female	94	5.3%
White female	Non-White female	52	1.9%
Non-White male	Non-White female	0	No data
White male	*White female*	*94*	*50.0%*
White female	White female	381	22.8%
Non-White female	White female	120	2.5%
Non-White male	White female	0	No data
White male	*White male*	*299*	*45.8%*
White female	White male	491	31.2%
Non-White female	White male	89	16.9%
Non-White male	White male	102	9.8%
White male	*Non-White female*	*10*	*40.0%*
Non-White female	Non-White female	94	5.3%
White female	Non-White female	52	1.9%
Non-White male	Non-White female	0	No data
White male	*Non-White male*	*54*	*20.4%*
White female	Non-White male	130	13.8%
Non-White female	Non-White male	131	7.6%
Non-White male	Non-White male	183	7.1%

Appendix I

The below chart was derived from the same data as the patient–therapist matching evaluating how many days patients remain in treatment. As the book discusses, days in treatment are associated with successful treatment completion rates. Just like high school graduation rates, students making it to their senior year are significantly more likely to successfully graduate. The goal for addiction treatment and high schools is to make sure the individuals remain engaged all the way to "graduation."

This chart shows the difference in number of days in treatment between White and non-White patients. This outcome is extremely troubling, but for some, not surprising.

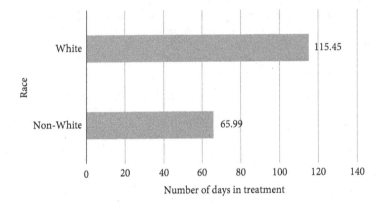

Appendix J

Below is a chart that shows our work with a local addiction treatment clinic. We pulled discharge data from their electronic health records system for this specific treatment location. Reasons for discharge varied across treatment systems with this program were several. Regardless, there was usually one positive reason for discharge, completing with staff approval, with the remaining reasons mostly negative. These negative reasons included patient dropout, patient withdrawing from services, patient noncompliance, and so on.

We were interested in increasing the percentage of completed with staff approval reason. Our dashboard technology tool, developed by Takoda, a startup in St. Louis, was introduced in March 2019. We requested discharge data for the 6 months prior to implementing the dashboard tool. The successful treatment rate hovered around 11 percent. Four months later, successful completion rates more than doubled to about 27 percent.

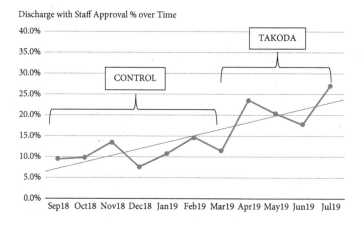

Discharge with Staff Approval % over Time

Appendix K

Below are screenshots of therapists' dashboards. Screenshot 1 allows the therapist the view of their caseload. Screenshot 2 is the view of the Dimensions of Recovery questions and how they are scored. Final Screenshot #3 shows a patient's recovery progress over time.

Screenshot 1

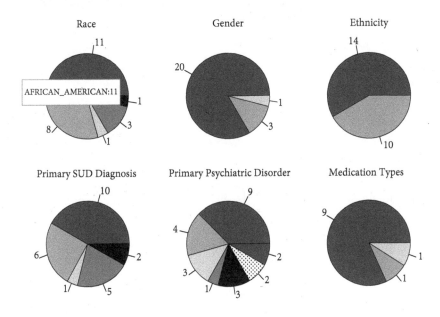

Screenshot 2

Strongly disagree	Disagree	Neither Agree nor Disagree	Agree	Strongly Agree
0 1 2	3 4	5	6 7	8 9 10

HEALTH
I believe that staying clean and sober will have a positive effect on my health.

Choose...
0
1
2
3
4
5
6
7
8
9
10

COMMUNITY
I am able to find people who are supportive of my efforts.

HOME
I live in a home that supports recovery.

PURPOSE
I have a job that I like.

MEDICATIONS
During the past week I took my medication as prescribed.

Choose...

CRAVINGS
In the last 24-48 hours I had no cravings

Choose...

Screenshot 3

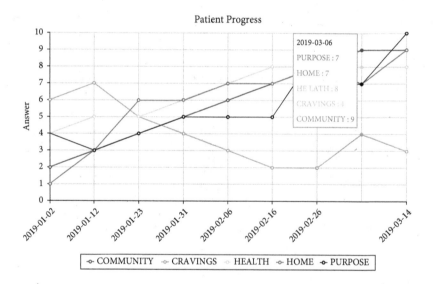

Patient Progress

2019-03-06
PURPOSE : 7
HOME : 7
HEALTH : 8
CRAVINGS : 4
COMMUNITY : 9

-o- COMMUNITY -o- CRAVINGS -o- HEALTH -o- HOME -o- PURPOSE

Bibliography

1. Bouchery EE, Harwood HJ, Sacks JJ, Simon CJ, Brewer RD. Economic costs of excessive alcohol consumption in the U.S., 2006. *Am J Prev Med*. 2011;*41*(5):516–524. doi:10.1016/j.amepre.2011.06.045
2. Substance Abuse and Mental Health Services Administration. *National Survey of Substance Abuse Treatment Services (N-SSATS): 2013: Data on Substance Abuse Treatment Facilities*. BHSIS Series S-73, HHS Publication No. (SMA) 14-4890. Rockville, MD: Substance Abuse and Mental Health Services Administration; 2014. http://wwwdasis.samhsa.gov/dasis2/nssats/2013_N-SSATS_National_Survey_of_ Substance_Abuse_Treatment_Services.pdf
3. Chambless DL, Hollon S. Defining empirically supported therapies. *J Consult Clin Psychol*. 1998;*66*(1):7–18.
4. National Institute on Drug Abuse. Adoption of NIDA's Evidence-Based Treatments in Real World Settings: A National Advisory Council on Drug Abuse Workgroup Report. 2012. https://www.apa.org/about/gr/science/spin/2012/09/evidence-based-treatments.pdf
5. Centers for Disease Control and Prevention. U.S. drug overdose deaths continue to rise; increase fueled by synthetic opioids. 2018. https://www.cdc.gov/media/releases/ 2018/p0329-drug-overdose-deaths.html
6. Scholl L, Seth P, Kariisa M, Wilson N, Baldwin G. Drug and opioid-involved overdose deaths—United States, 2013–2017. *MMWR Morb Mortal Wkly Rep*. 2018;*67*(5152):1419–1427. doi:10.15585/mmwr.mm675152e1
7. Mokdad AH, Marks JS, Stroup DF, Gerberding JL. Actual causes of death in the United States, 2000. *JAMA*. 2004;*291*(10):1238–1245. doi:10.1001/jama.291.10.1238
8. International Wines and Spirits Record. Worldwide alcohol consumption declines— 1.6 percent. 2019. https://www.theiwsr.com/wp-content/uploads/Press-Release-IWSR-Releases-New-Global-Data_29May19.pdf
9. National Institute on Drug Abuse. Trends & statistics. 2017. https://www.drugabuse. gov/related-topics/trends-statistics. Accessed October 15, 2019.
10. Witkiewitz K, Litten RZ, Leggio L. Advances in the science and treatment of alcohol use disorder. *Sci Adv*. 2019;*5*(9), eaax4043. doi:10.1126/sciadv.aax4043
11. Ducci F, Goldman D. Genetic approaches to addiction: genes and alcohol. *Addiction*. 2008;*103*(9):1414–1428. doi:10.1111/j.1360-0443.2008.02203.x
12. Substance Abuse and Mental Health Services Administration. *More than 7 million children live with a parent with alcohol problems. Data Spotlight*. 2012. https:// www.samhsa.gov/data/sites/default/files/Spot061ChildrenOfAlcoholics2012/ Spot061ChildrenOfAlcoholics2012.pdf
13. White HR, Johnson V, Buyske S. Parental modeling and parenting behavior effects on offspring alcohol and cigarette use: a growth curve analysis. *J Subst Abuse*. 2000;*12*(3):287–310. doi:10.1016/S0899-3289(00)00056-0

14. Substance Abuse and Mental Health Services Administration. *Results from the 2012 National Survey on Drug Use and Health: Summary of National Findings*. 2013.

15. Substance Abuse and Mental Health Administration. *Results From the 2015 National Survey on Drug Use and Health: Detailed Tables*. 2016. http://www.samhsa.gov/data/sites/default/files/NSDUH-DetTabs-2015/NSDUH-DetTabs-2015/NSDUH-DetTabs-2015.htm#tab2-19b

16. Centers for Disease Control and Prevention. Alcohol use and health. 2018. https://www.cdc.gov/alcohol/fact-sheets/alcohol-use.htm. Accessed October 15, 2019.

17. Fox K. Arlington police release incident report in Six Flags death. *NBCDFW News*. 2013, November 8. https://www.nbcdfw.com/news/local/arlington-police-release-incident-report-in-six-flags-death/1962562/

18. Huang Y-H, Lee T-C, Lee T-H, et al. Thirty-day mortality in traumatically brain-injured patients undergoing decompressive craniectomy. *J Neurosurg*. 2013;*118*(6). https://thejns.org/view/journals/j-neurosurg/118/6/article-p1329.xml. Accessed January 4, 2020.

19. Jalbert JJ, Nguyen LL, Gerhard-Herman MD, et al. Outcomes after carotid artery stenting in Medicare beneficiaries, 2005 to 2009. *JAMA Neurol*. 2015;*72*(3):276–286. doi:10.1001/jamaneurol.2014.3638

20. Crow SJ, Peterson CB, Swanson SA, et al. Increased mortality in bulimia nervosa and other eating disorders. *Am J Psychiatry*. 2009;*166*(12):1342–1346. doi:10.1176/appi.ajp.2009.09020247

21. Brorson HH, Ajo Arnevik E, Rand-Hendriksen K, Duckert F. Drop-out from addiction treatment: a systematic review of risk factors. *Clin Psychol Rev*. 2013;*33*(8):1010–1024.

22. Patterson Silver Wolf DA, van den Berk-Clark C, Williams SL, Dulmus CN. Are therapists likely to use a new empirically supported treatment if required? *J Soc Work*. 2018;*18*(6):666–678. doi:10.1177/1468017317743138

23. Dalsbo TD, Hammerstrøm TK, Vist GE, et al. Psychosocial interventions for retention in drug abuse treatment. *Cochrane Database Syst Rev*. 2016. doi:10.1002/14651858.CD008220.pub2

24. López-Goñi JJ, Fernández-Montalvo J, Cacho R, Arteaga A. Profile of addicted patients who reenter treatment programs. *Subst Abus*. 2014;*35*:176–183.

25. Howard KI, Kopta MS, Krause MS, Orlinsky DE. The dose–effect relationship in psychotherapy. *Am Psychol*. 1986;*41*:159–164.

26. Stark MJ. Dropping out of substance abuse treatment: a clinically oriented review. *Clin Psychol Rev*. 1992;*12*:93–116.

27. Eaton L. Numbers starting treatment for drug misuse increase by 20 percent over two years. *BMJ*. 2004;*392*(7474):1066.

28. Hawkins EJ, Baer JS, Kivlahan DR. Concurrent monitoring of psychological distress and satisfaction measures as predictors of addiction treatment retention. *J Subst Abuse Treat*. 2008;*35*:207–216.

29. Barreno EM, Domínguez-Salas S, Díaz-Batanero C, Lozano ÓM, Marín JAL, Verdejo-García A. Specific aspects of cognitive impulsivity are longitudinally associated with lower treatment retention and greater relapse in therapeutic community treatment. *J Subst Abuse Treat*. 2019;*96*:33–38. doi:10.1016/j.jsat.2018.10.004

30. Miller WR, Walters ST, Bennett ME. How effective is alcoholism treatment in the United States? *J Stud Alcohol*. 2001;*62*(2):211–220. doi:10.15288/jsa.2001.62.211

31. Patterson Silver Wolf DA, Dulmus CN, Maguin E, Linn BK, Hales T. Therapist-patient demographic profile matching: a move toward performance-based practice. *Res Soc Work Pract.* 2019;*29*(6). doi:10.1177/1049731518783582

32. Johnson K, Rigg KK, Hopkins Eyles C. Receiving addiction treatment in the U.S.: do patient demographics, drug of choice, or substance use disorder severity matter? *Int J Drug Policy.* 2020;*75*:102583. doi:10.1016/j.drugpo.2019.10.009

33. Pew Research Center. Many Americans say made-up news is a critical problem that needs to be fixed. 2019, June 5. https://www.journalism.org/2019/06/05/many-americans-say-made-up-news-is-a-critical-problem-that-needs-to-be-fixed/. Accessed December 11, 2020.

34. Patterson Silver Wolf DA. Real-time data: as vital for opioid overdose deaths as for Covid-19. *Stat News.* 2020. https://www.statnews.com/2020/05/20/real-time-data-essential-for-opioid-overdose-crisis-as-for-covid-19/. Accessed December 11, 2020.

35. Guo J. The disease killing White Americans goes way deeper than opioids. *Washington Post.* 2017, March 4. https://www.washingtonpost.com/news/wonk/wp/2017/03/24/the-disease-killing-white-americans-goes-way-deeper-than-opioids/

36. Connors GJ, Rychtarik RG. The Supreme Court VA/disease model case: background and implications. *Psychol Addict Behav.* 1988;*2*(3):101–107. doi:10.1037/h0080558

37. Blocker JS. Did prohibition really work? Alcohol prohibition as a public health innovation. *Am J Public Health.* 2006;*96*(2):233–243. doi:10.2105/AJPH.2005.065409

38. McClellan ML. Historical perspectives on alcoholism treatment for women in the United States, 1870–1990. *Alcohol Treat Q.* 2011;*29*(4):332–356. doi:10.1080/07347324.2011.608597

39. American Psychiatric Association. *Diagnostic and Statistical Manual of Mental Disorders, Fifth Edition (DSM-5).* Washington, DC: American Psychiatric Publishing; 2013.

40. U.S. Department of Health & Human Services. *Facing Addiction in America: The Surgeon General's Report on Alcohol, Drugs, and Health.* U.S. Department of Health and Human Services; 2016. https://www.ncbi.nlm.nih.gov/books/NBK424857/pdf/Bookshelf_NBK424857.pdf. Accessed December 11, 2020.

41. Chambless DL, Hollon SD. Defining empirically supported therapies. *J Consult Clin Psychol.* 1998;*66*(1):7–18. doi:10.1037/0022-006X.66.1.7

42. Rogers C. *Client-Centered Therapy.* Cambridge, MA: Riverside Press; 1951.

43. Rogers EM. *Diffusion of Innovations.* 5th ed. New York: Free Press; 2003.

44. Rogers C. *Counseling and Psychotherapy.* Cambridge, MA: Riverside Press; 1942.

45. Miller WR, Moyers TB. Motivational interviewing and the clinical science of Carl Rogers. *J Consult Clin Psychol.* 2017;*85*(8):757–766. doi:10.1037/ccp0000179

46. Zweben A, Zuckoff A. Motivational interviewing and treatment adherence. In: Miller WR, Rollnick S, eds. *Motivational Interviewing: Preparing People for Change* (2nd ed.). New York: Guilford Press; 2002.

47. Project MATCH Research Group. Project MATCH: Rationale and methods for a multisite clinical trial matching patients to alcoholism treatment. *Alcohol Clin Exp Res.* 1993;*17*:1130–1145.

48. Project MATCH Research Group. Matching alcoholism treatments to client heterogeneity: Project MATCH posttreatment drinking outcomes. *J Stud Alcohol.* 1997;*58*(1):7–29.

49. Miller WR, Rollnick S. *Motivational Interviewing: Preparing People to Change Addictive Behavior.* New York: Guilford Press; 1991.

50. Glaser FB. The unsinkable Project MATCH. *Addiction.* 1999;*94*(1):34–36.
51. Prochaska JO, DiClemente CC, Norcross JC. In search of how people change: applications to addictive behaviors. *Am Psychol.* 1992;*47*(9):1102–1114.
52. Butler AC, Chapman JE, Forman EM, Beck AT. The empirical status of cognitive-behavioral therapy: a review of meta-analyses. *Clin Psychol Rev.* 2006;*26*(1):17–31. doi:10.1016/j.cpr.2005.07.003
53. Greenwood JD. Understanding the "cognitive revolution" in psychology. *J Hist Behav Sci.* 1999;*35*(1):1–22. doi:10.1002/(SICI)1520-6696(199924)35: 1<1::AID-JHBS1>3.0.CO;2-4
54. McHugh RK, Hearon BA, Otto MW. Cognitive behavioral therapy for substance use disorders. *Psychiatr Clin North Am.* 2010;*33*(3):511–525. doi:10.1016/j.psc.2010.04.012
55. Leach B, Norris JL. Factors in the development of Alcoholics Anonymous (AA). In: *The Biology of Alcoholism.* New York: Springer; 1977:441–543. doi:10.1007/978-1-4613-4199-4_11
56. Cantril H. *The Psychology of Social Movements.* New York: Wiley; 1941.
57. Nowinski J, Baker S, Carroll K. *Twelve Step Facilitation Therapy Manual: A Clinical Research Guide for Therapists Treating Individuals With Alcohol Abuse and Dependence.* Rockville, MD: National Institute on Alcohol Abuse and Alcoholism; 1992.
58. Miller PG, Miller WR. What should we be aiming for in the treatment of addiction? *Addiction.* 2009;*104*(5):685–686.
59. Brown SA, Glasner-Edwards SV, Tate SR, McQuaid JR, Chalekian J, Granholm E. Integrated cognitive behavioral therapy versus twelve-step facilitation therapy for substance-dependent adults with depressive disorders. *J Psychoactive Drugs.* 2006;*38*(4):449–460. doi:10.1080/02791072.2006.10400584
60. Institute of Medicine. *Improving the Quality of Health Care for Mental and Substance-Use Conditions: Quality Chasm Series.* Vol. 77–139. Washington, DC: National Academy Press Report; 2006.
61. Morgenstern J. Effective technology transfer in alcoholism treatment. *Subst Use Misuse.* 2000;*35*:1659–1678.
62. Patterson Silver Wolf DA. Factors influencing the implementation of a brief alcohol screening and educational intervention in social settings not specializing in addiction services. *Soc Work Health Care.* 2015;*54*(4):345–364. doi:10.1080/00981389.2015.1005270
63. Glisson C, Landsverk J, Schoenwald S, et al. Assessing the organizational social context (OSC) of mental health services: implications for research and practice. *Adm Policy Ment Health.* 2008;*35*:98–113.
64. Glisson C. The organizational context of children's mental health services. *Clin Child Fam Psychol Rev.* 2002;*5*:233–253.
65. Glisson C, Green P, Williams N. Assessing the organizational social context (OSC) of child welfare systems: implications for research and practice. *Child Abuse Negl.* 2012;*36*:621–632.
66. Patterson Silver Wolf DA, Dulmus CN, Maguin E, Fava N. Refining the Evidence-Based Practice Attitude Scale: an alternative confirmatory factor analysis. *Soc Work Res.* 2014;*38*(1):47–58. doi:10.1093/swr/svu006
67. Aarons GA. Mental health provider attitudes toward adoption of evidence-based practice: the Evidence-Based Practice Attitude Scale (EBPAS). *Ment Health Serv Res.* 2004;*6*:61–74.

68. Patterson Silver Wolf DA, Maguin E, Dulmus CN, Nisbet BC. Individual worker-level attitudes toward empirically supported treatments. *Res Soc Work Pract.* 2013;*23*(1):95–99. doi:10.1177/1049731512463442

69. Patterson Silver Wolf DA, Dulmus CN, Maguin E, Cristalli ME. Factors influencing worker morale: evaluating provider demographics, workplace environment and using ESTs. *Res Soc Work Pract.* 2013;*23*(3):302–308.

70. Patterson Silver Wolf DA, Dulmus CN, Maguin E. Is openness to using empirically supported treatments related to organizational culture and climate? *J Soc Serv Res.* 2013;*39*(4):562–571. http://search.ebscohost.com/login.aspx?direct=true&db=cmed m&AN=24159247&site=ehost-live&scope=site

71. Patterson Silver Wolf DA, Dulmus CN, Maguin E. Empirically supported treatment's impact on organizational culture and climate. *Res Soc Work Pract.* 2012;*22*(6):665–671. doi:10.1177/1049731512448934

72. Patterson Silver Wolf DA, Dulmus CN, Maguin E, Cristalli M. Do organizational culture and climate matter for successful client outcomes? *Res Soc Work Pract.* 2014;*24*(6):670–675. doi:10.1177/1049731513506616

73. Patterson Silver Wolf DA, Dulmus CN, Maguin E, Perkins JD. Differential outcomes in agency-based mental health care between minority and majority youth. *Res Soc Work Pract.* 2014;*26*(3):260–265. doi:10.1177/1049731514550208

74. Glisson C. Personal communication. Patterson Silver Wolf DA, ed. 2007.

75. Patterson Silver Wolf D, Dulmus CN, Maguin E. Empirically supported treatment's impact on organizational culture and climate. *Res Soc Work Pract.* 2012;*22*(6):665–671.

76. Patterson Silver Wolf DA, Dulmus CN, Maguin E, Fava N. Refining the evidence-based practice attitude scale: an alternative confirmatory factor analysis. *Soc Work Res.* 2014;*38*(1):47–58. doi:10.1093/swr/svu006

77. Dulmus CN, Patterson Silver Wolf DA, Maguin E, Kessler J. Relationship between youth restraint and work environment. In: *20th SSWR Annual Conference.* Washington, DC; 2016.

78. David A. Patterson, Silver Wolf (Adelv unegv Waya), Travis W. Hales, Eugene Maguin, Catherine N. Dulmus. Research-supported treatment and organizational culture and climate's impact on child welfare outcomes. 2017;*28*(7):869–875.. https:// doi.org/10.1177/1049731517697131

79. Barrick MR, Mount MK. Yes, personality matters: moving on to more important matters. *Hum Perform.* 2005;*18*:359–372.

80. Patterson Silver Wolf DA. What are the ideal characteristics of empirically supported treatment adopters? *J Hum Behav Soc Environ.* 2014;*24*(3):408–414. doi:10.1080/ 10911359.2014.875343

81. Proctor EK, Landsverk J, Aarons G, Chambers D, Glisson C, Mittman B. Implementation research in mental health services: an emerging science with conceptual, methodological, and training challenges. *Adm Policy Ment Heal.* 2009;*36*(1):24–34. doi:10.1007/s10488-008-0197-4

82. Patterson Silver Wolf DA, Linn BK, Dulmus CN. Are grittier front-line therapists more likely to implement evidence-based interventions? *Community Ment Health J.* 2018;*54*(7):959–966. doi:10.1007/s10597-018-0305-1

83. Patterson Silver Wolf DA, Maguin E, Ramsey AT, Stringfellow E. Measuring attitudes toward empirically supported treatment in real-world addiction services. *J Soc Work Pract Addict.* 2014;*14*(2):141–154. doi:10.1080/1533256X.2014.902717

84. Klein KJ, Knight AP. Innovation implementation: overcoming the challenge. *Curr Dir Psychol Sci.* 2005;*14*(5):243–246. doi:10.1111/j.0963-7214.2005.00373.x

85. Patterson Silver Wolf DA, BlackDeer AA, Beeler-Stinn S, Zheng K, Stazrad K. Performance-based practice: clinical dashboards for addiction treatment retention. *Res Soc Work Pract.* 2021;*80*:6–13. doi:10.1177/1049731520972798

86. Schuchat A, Houry D, Guy GP. New data on opioid use and prescribing in the United States. *JAMA.* 2017;*318*(5):425–426. doi:10.1001/jama.2017.8913

87. National Academies of Science. *Medications for Opioid Use Disorder Save Lives.* Washington, DC: National Academies Press; 2019. doi:10.17226/25310

88. Williams AR, Samples H, Crystal S, Olfson M. Acute care, prescription opioid use, and overdose following discontinuation of long-term buprenorphine treatment for opioid use disorder. *Am J Psychiatry.* 2020;*177*(2):117–124. doi:10.1176/appi.ajp.2019.19060612

89. Sutherland CAM, Rhodes G, Burton NS, Young AW. Do facial first impressions reflect a shared social reality? *Br J Psychol.* 2019;*12390*:1–19. doi:10.1111/bjop.12390

90. Mileva M, Young AW, Kramer RSS, Burton AM. Understanding facial impressions between and within identities. *Cognition.* 2019;*190*:184–198. doi:10.1016/j.cognition.2019.04.027

91. South Palomares JK, Sutherland CAM, Young AW. Facial first impressions and partner preference models: comparable or distinct underlying structures? *Br J Psychol.* 2018;*109*(3):538–563. doi:10.1111/bjop.12286

92. Kret ME. The role of pupil size in communication. Is there room for learning? *Cogn Emot.* 2018;*32*(5):1139–1145. doi:10.1080/02699931.2017.1370417

93. Rogers CR. Empathic: an unappreciated way of being. *Couns Psychol.* 1975;*5*(2):2–10. doi:10.1177/001100007500500202

94. Feller CP, Cottone RR. The importance of empathy in the therapeutic alliance. *J Humanist Couns Educ Dev.* 2003;*42*(1):53–61. doi:10.1002/j.2164-490x.2003.tb00168.x

95. Mercer SW, Reynolds WJ. Empathy and quality of care. *Br J Gen Pract.* 2002;*52*(Suppl):9–11.

96. Clark MA, Robertson MM, Young S. "I feel your pain": a critical review of organizational research on empathy. *J Organ Behav.* 2019;*40*(2):166–192. doi:10.1002/job.2348

97. Moyers TB, Miller WR. Is low therapist empathy toxic? *Psychol Addict Behav.* 2013;*27*(3):878–884. doi:10.1037/a0030274

98. Miller WR, Baca LM. Two-year follow-up of bibliotherapy and therapist-directed controlled drinking training for problem drinkers. *Behav Ther.* 1983;*14*(3):441–448. doi:10.1016/S0005-7894(83)80107-5

99. Miller WR, Taylor CA, West JC. Focused versus broad-spectrum behavior therapy for problem drinkers. *J Consult Clin Psychol.* 1980;*48*(5):590–601.

100. Norcross JC, Lambert MJ. Psychotherapy relationships that work II. *Psychotherapy.* 2011;*48*(1):4–8. doi:10.1037/a0022180

101. Searles HF. Concerning transference and countertransference. *Psychoanal Dialogues.* 2017;*27*(2):192–210. doi:10.1080/10481885.2017.1285167

102. Anderson T, Crowley MEJ, Himawan L, Holmberg JK, Uhlin BD. Therapist facilitative interpersonal skills and training status: a randomized clinical trial on alliance and outcome. *Psychother Res.* 2016;*26*(5):511–529. doi:10.1080/10503307.2015.1049671

103. Najavits LM, Weiss RD. Variations in therapist effectiveness in the treatment of patients with substance use disorders: an empirical review. *Addiction.* 1994;89(6):679–688. doi:10.1111/j.1360-0443.1994.tb00954.x

104. Machell DF. Counselor substance abuse history, client fellowship, and alcoholism treatment outcome. Brief report. 1987. https://files.eric.ed.gov/fulltext/ED297225.pdf. Accessed February 15, 2020.

105. Crits-Christoph P, Hamilton JL, Ring-Kurtz S, et al. Program, counselor, and patient variability in the alliance: a multilevel study of the alliance in relation to substance use outcomes. *J Subst Abuse Treat.* 2011;40(4):405–413. doi:10.1016/j.jsat.2011.01.003

106. Fiorentine R, Hillhouse MP. Drug treatment effectiveness and client-counselor empathy: exploring the effects of gender and ethnic congruency. *J Drug Issues.* 1999;29(1):59–74. doi:10.1177/002204269902900104

107. Sterling RC, Gottheil E, Weinstein SP, Serota R. The effect of therapist/patient race- and sex-matching in individual treatment. *Addiction.* 2001;96(7):1015–1022. doi:10.1046/j.1360-0443.2001.967101511.x

108. Sterling RC, Gottheil E, Weinstein SP, Serota R. Therapist/patient race and sex matching: treatment retention and 9-month follow-up outcome. *Addiction.* 1998;93(7):1043–1050. doi:10.1046/j.1360-0443.1998.93710439.x

109. Ruglass LM, Hien DA, Hu MC, et al. Racial/ethnic match and treatment outcomes for women with PTSD and substance use disorders receiving community-based treatment. *Community Ment Health J.* 2014;50(7):811–822. doi:10.1007/s10597-014-9732-9

110. Wintersteen MB, Mensinger JL, Diamond GS. Do gender and racial differences between patient and therapist affect therapeutic alliance and treatment retention in adolescents? *Prof Psychol Res Pract.* 2005;36(4):400–408. doi:10.1037/0735-7028.36.4.400

111. Patterson Silver Wolf D, Dulmus CN, Maguin E, Linn BK, Hales TW. Therapist-patient demographic profile matching: a movement toward performance-based practice. *Res Soc Work Pract.* 2019;29(6):677–683. doi:10.1177/1049731518783582

112. Perkins KS, Tharp BE, Ramsey AT, Patterson Silver Wolf DA. Mapping the evidence to improve retention rates in addiction services. *J Soc Work Pract Addict.* 2016;16(3):233–251. doi:10.1080/1533256X.2016.1200055

113. Patterson Silver Wolf DA. Motivational interviewing: does it increase retention in outpatient treatment? *Subst Abus.* 2008;29(1):17–23.

114. Vaillant GE. A 60-year follow-up of alcoholic men. *Addiction.* 2003;98(8):1043–1051. doi:10.1046/j.1360-0443.2003.00422.x

115. Scott CK, Dennis ML, Laudet A, Funk RR, Simeone RS. Surviving drug addiction: the effect of treatment and abstinence on mortality. *Am J Public Health.* 2011;101:737–744.

116. Talbott GD. The disabled doctors program of Georgia. *Alcohol Clin Exp Res.* 1977;1(2):143–146. doi:10.1111/j.1530-0277.1977.tb05862.x

117. DuPont RL, McLellan AT, White WL, Merlo LJ, Gold MS. Setting the standard for recovery: physicians' health programs. *J Subst Abuse Treat.* 2009;36(2):159–171. doi:10.1016/j.jsat.2008.01.004

118. McLellan AT, Skipper GS, Campbell M, DuPont RL. Five year outcomes in a cohort study of physicians treated for substance use disorders in the United States. *BMJ.* 2008;337(7679):1154–1156. doi:10.1136/bmj.a2038

119. Dowding D, Randell R, Gardner P, et al. Dashboards for improving patient care: review of the literature. *Int J Med Inform.* 2015;*84*(2):87–100. doi:10.1016/j.ijmedinf.2014.10.001

120. Amarasingham R, Plantinga L, Diener-West M, Gaskin DJ, Powe NR. Clinical information technologies and inpatient outcomes: a multiple hospital study. *Arch Intern Med.* 2009;*169*(2):108–114. doi:10.1001/archinternmed.2008.520

121. Pauwels K, Ambler T, Clark BH, et al. Dashboards as a service: why, what, how, and what research is needed? *J Serv Res.* 2009;*12*(2):175–189. doi:10.1177/1094670509344213

122. Daley K, Richardson J, James I, Chambers A, Corbett D. Clinical dashboard: use in older adult mental health wards. *Psychiatrist.* 2013;*37*(3):85–88. doi:10.1192/pb.bp.111.035899

123. Strashny A. *Recovery Services Provided by Substance Abuse Treatment Facilities in the United States.* Substance Abuse and Mental Health Services Administration. 2013. http://www.ncbi.nlm.nih.gov/pubmed/27656736. Accessed March 4, 2020.

124. Pew Research Center. Mobile fact sheet. 2019. https://www.pewresearch.org/internet/fact-sheet/mobile/. Accessed March 19, 2020.

125. Kahneman D, Krueger AB, Schkade DA, Schwarz N, Stone AA. A survey method for characterizing daily life experience: the day reconstruction method. *Science.* 2004;*306*(5702):1776–1780.

126. Shiffman S, Stone AA, Hufford MR. Ecological momentary assessment. *Annu Rev Clin Psychol.* 2008;4:1–32.

127. Durkin K, Wolfe SE, May RW. Social bond theory and drunk driving in a sample of college students. *Coll Stud J.* 2007;*41*:734–744.

128. Hirschi T. *Causes of Delinquency.* Berkeley: University of California Press; 1969.

129. Bachman JG, Wallace JM, O'Malley PM, Johnston LD, Kurth CL, Neighbors HW. Racial/ethnic differences in smoking, drinking, and illicit drug use among American high school seniors, 1976–89. *Am J Public Health.* 1991;*81*:372–377.

130. Wallace JM, Muroff JR. Preventing substance abuse among African American children and youth: race differences in risk factor exposure and vulnerability. *J Prim Prev.* 2002;*22*:235–261.

131. Jenson J, Fraser M. *Social Policy for Children and Families: A Risk and Resilience Perspective.* Thousand Oaks, CA: Sage; 2005.

132. Plybon LE, Edwards L, Butler D, Belgrave FZ, Allison F. Examining the link between neighborhood cohesion and school outcomes: the role of support coping among African American adolescent girls. *J Black Psychol.* 2003;*24*(4):393–407.

133. Hendershot C, Witkiewitz K, George W, Marlatt G. Relapse prevention for addictive behaviors. *Subst Abuse Treat Prev Policy.* 2011;*6*(17):1–17.

134. Marlatt GA, George WH. Relapse prevention: introduction and overview of the model. *Br J Addict.* 1984;*79*(3):261–273.

135. Walton MA, Blow FC, Bingham CR, Chermack ST. Individual and social/environmental predictors of alcohol and drug use 2 years following substance abuse treatment. *Addict Behav.* 2003;*28*(4):627–642.

136. DuPont RL, McLellan AT, Carr G, Gendel M, Skipper GE. How are addicted physicians treated? A national survey of physician health programs. *J Subst Abuse Treat.* 2009;*37*(1):1–7. doi:10.1016/j.jsat.2009.03.010

137. Looby A, De Young KP, Earleywine M. Challenges expectancies to prevent non-medical prescription stimulant use: a randomized, controlled trial. *Drug Alcohol Depend.* 2013;*132*:362–368.

138. Hansen WB, Dusenbury L, Bishop D, Derzon JH. Substance abuse prevention program content: systematizing the classification of what programs target for change. *Health Educ Res.* 2007;*22*(3):351–360.

139. Sandler I, Wolchik SA, Cruden G, et al. Overview of meta-analyses of the prevention of mental health, substance use, and conduct problems. *Annu Rev Clin Psychol.* 2014;*10*(1):243–273.

140. Ajzen I, Fishbein M. *Understanding Attitudes and Predicting Social Behavior.* Englewood Cliffs, NJ: Prentice Hall; 1980.

141. Fishbein M, Ajzen I. *Predicting and Changing Behavior: A Reasoned Action Approach.* New York: Taylor & Francis; 2010.

142. Fishbein M, Yzer M. Using theory to design effective health behavior interventions. *Commun Theory.* 2003;*13*(2):164–183.

Index

For the benefit of digital users, indexed terms that span two pages (e.g., 52–53) may, on occasion, appear on only one of those pages.